The Terrible Power of a Minor Guilt

The Terrible Power
of a Minor Guilt

❧❧❧

LITERARY ESSAYS

Abraham B. Yehoshua

Translated from the Hebrew by Ora Cummings

Syracuse University Press

First Edition 2000
00 01 02 03 04 05   6 5 4 3 2 1

Originally published in Hebrew as *Kohah ha-nora shel ashmah ketanah:
ha-heksher ha-musari shel ha-tekst ha-sifruti*.
Tel Aviv: Yediot aharonot: Sifre hemed, 1998.

The paper used in this publication meets the minimum requirements of
American National Standard for Information Sciences—Permanence of
Paper for Printed Library Materials, ANSI Z39.48–1984. ∞™

Library of Congress Cataloging-in-Publication Data
Yehoshua, Abraham B.
[Essays. English. Selections]
The terrible power of a minor guilt : literary essays / A.B. Yehoshua ; translated from
the Hebrew by Ora Cummings.
p. cm.
ISBN 0-8156-0656-7 (alk. paper)
1. Ethics in literature.   2. Literature—Aesthetics.   3. Guilt in literature.   I. Cummings,
Ora.   II. Title.
PN49 .Y4413 2000
809'.93353—dc21   00-030086

Manufactured in the United States of America

Contents

Introduction

I have been troubled for some time, both as a writer and as a reader and teacher of literature, by questions concerning the relationship between art in general—literature, theater, and cinema, in particular—and what we tend to define as the field of morality, ethics, or moral values (terms for which I shall shortly attempt to supply more accurate definitions). It has been difficult in recent years to find in written critiques of novels, stories, plays, or even films a direct reference to the moral issues raised by the work or to the writer's good or bad moral judgment or to the behavior of the characters in the work. Very rarely, nowadays, are we able to hear a reader's cry of protest or wonder at the moral stance taken by a character or author in a work of literature. Even more rarely is it possible to find a reader or a critic bold enough to tie his protest or wonder to an aesthetic evaluation of the work. The most common words in the language of criticism, both professional and private, in evaluating a literary work are *credibility, complexity, depth* and—especially—*novelty*. Only very infrequently is it possible to find words such as *moral, value, right,* and *good*.

In the second chapter of his excellent book *The Company We Keep* (1988), Wayne C. Booth bemoans how difficult it is for modern literary critics when they try to discuss the moral aspects of a work of prose. Booth's claim is that among all the various schools of thought, not one exists that dares to define itself as *moral criticism*. Although here and there one can find moral references under various headings, the fact remains that these references must be hidden behind or annexed to discussions bearing different titles—such as *political, social, cultural, psychological,* or *psychoanalytical*—or to discussions dealing with reader response, feminist commentary, or the text's discourse of power, which serves to prove the extent to which straightforward and open discussion on the moral aspects of a text has become problematic and unfashionable.

Mr. Booth is right to be surprised. Indeed, until the end of the nineteenth century, all lovers of literature expected a clear-cut regard for the moral values presented in a piece of literature and saw no reason to conceal the moral issue under such neutral terms as *significant shape* or *aesthetic integrity.*

And Mr. Booth continues to ponder the various reasons behind the growing trend among modern critics not to deal openly with the moral and ethical values presented by a literary piece and to avoid open moral criticism of the values expressed both by the author and by his or her characters. But before summing up briefly some of Mr. Booth's observations and trying to add some of my own, I think I should attempt to explain the terms *morality* or *value judgment,* which I will use throughout the length of this essay.

When I began writing this book, I did not imagine that I would have to start off by supplying explanations or definitions for the term *value/moral judgment,* which is part of my own day-to-day language. After showing the manuscript to several of my colleagues, however, it became apparent to me that when people leave the level of day-to-day language—where any layman can understand a sentence such as, "It's not very moral of you to keep me waiting in the street for half an hour"—and move on to a more theoretical and abstract discussion, there arises a need to define the term *morality,* which seems to have suffered some bad battering, not to mention confusion and even disintegration, at the hands of the postmodernists, pluralists, and propounders of relativity, who have fondled it freely and generally turned it inside out and upside down. Indeed, it is difficult these days for one to say the words *moral* and *ethical* without immediately being attacked with, "And exactly whose morals are you referring to? After all, everyone has his own morals," or more gently, "You can call it moral or immoral, but I don't think it's a question of morals at all."

What, then, is moral? And what will be the meaning of *moral statement* or *moral relations* as they appear in the following discussions? When are we going to be able to say that a particular sentence is a moral statement, and when are we not? Is it enough to say that any sentence that necessarily refers to questions of good or bad in interpersonal relations is a sentence to which we can relate a moral meaning? I stress the word *necessarily* on the assumption that many sentences can include the words *good* or *bad*, but these words are not necessary to the subject under discussion, and they can be replaced by other words. It may be said, for example, "It's good to warm up the car's engine before setting off on a journey." But the word *good* in this sentence is not necessarily essential, and it can be replaced by *worthwhile*, or *wise*, or *important*, and so on. Whereas in a moral sentence, such as "murder is a bad act," there is no possibility of replacing the word *bad* with another and of saying, "it is worthwhile not to murder" or "it is important not to murder" or "it would be wise not to murder." But would this differentiation really be sufficient to give us a clear model regarding the question of when we are presenting moral images and when we are not?

A simple suggestion might be useful here: every image or statement that contains a demand for absoluteness and generality—that signals to an individual what he or she must and must not do with regard to human relations—is of moral significance. The basic point in this definition consists of a demand for absolutness and generality. In other words, the moral statement incorporates a demand whose force lies in the fact that it does not relate to a personal issue ("don't murder me" or "don't steal from him"); rather, it is a general demand that is unbound by time or person—"do not murder," "honor your father and your mother," or in less dramatic instances, "bury the dead" or "do not endanger your peer's life." "Do not murder" is a sentence that consists of a demand that is all-encompassing, and anyone who accepts it says murder is and always has been a bad and immoral act, even when it took place among the cave-dwelling hunters thousands of years ago and even when it happened within human societies in which murder was accepted and tolerated. The same applies to cases in which murder will take place among the inhabitants of Mars and Jupiter in another thousand years, even if the laws there are different. Nonetheless, it is possible for every all-inclusive moral or ethical perception to have its own reservations in keeping with this or that situation—such as, "it is permitted and even desirable for one to kill someone who intends to kill us" or "it is permissible to kill the murderer who has already committed murder" or "it is permissible and perhaps even ethical to confiscate the bag of heroin from a drug dealer." However, even these reservations, which present other moral issues, have to conform to general criteria. The killing of a man who came to kill you is moral even if it was carried out a thousand years ago or will happen in another thousand years, everywhere and in any human society.

Two reasons brought me to accommodate my colleagues by trying to make this terminological clarification, to make it obvious—in a singularly elementary way, and rightly so—to a not inconsiderable number of readers who take in-depth moral discussions seriously. One of these reasons is that from here on the pages of this book are going to be filled with such expressions as *moral/ethical behavior, moral map, moral values, moral/ethical skepticism, moral reproach,* and many others, and anyone who insists on misconstruing their meaning because of an inability (real or affected) to define the terms *ethics* or *morality,* well, I believe that I have placed in his or her hands at least one anchor to grasp hold of. But as far as I am concerned, the second reason is even more important. Moral visualization is first and foremost a *personal* visualization. It is not an anthropological or historical description, nor is it philosophical or religious; it is a personal stance. One can sum up what one considers to be the basic moral values of the Israelis or explain moral concepts as they appears in the New Testament. One can make sarcastic comments on the double standards of the French or the British and, of course, lecture on Kant and his moral theory, and one would still be merely dealing with matters concerning morality but not determining a moral attitude to the world and certainly not carrying out moral or ethical acts. It is only when one is required to air one's personal opinion (which can, if one so chooses, be based on this or that theory of morality and even be taken from it) and present it as a universal and binding principal, that it is possible to say that one is expressing a moral stance.

Let us return to the reasons for the difficulty suffered by modern-day literary criticism in dealing openly with moral judgment of literary works and in more detailed and profound discussions of the moral relations between characters appearing in works of prose, cinema, and theater at a time when there is prolific general academic activity in this field. As Wayne Booth says,

> Ethical inquiry of certain kinds is now quite fashionable. Though our culture is often described as having lost all faith in values, it nevertheless produces theories of ethics and morality at a great pace. It is true that many of our major novelists and poets have portrayed a world in which all honest thinkers admit that we are a forlorn race, lost in a cosmos indifferent to our ends, rootless, groundless, unaided by any rationally defensible code, expressing at best our irrational values in existential protest." (38)

And here, notwithstanding the fact that this picture often arises from literature and the literary criticism that deals with it, there is at the same time widespread activity on the part of philosophers who recoil from this worldview and publish additional proof that it is indeed possible to give rational explanations to moral allegations. A respectable number of books are being published under titles such as *The Theory of Ethics, The Logic of Ethics, Basic Premises of Moral Allegations,* and so on. In the meantime, new and special schools of thought are formed that deal, for example, with medical ethics, judiciary ethics, or the ethics of using nuclear power. Detailed moral discussions are held on ecological issues, social and psychological services, and more.

Thus, the issue returns to first base: Why does literary criticism, both professional and lay, withdraw from moral discussions or at least hesitate to speak out? And why has literature itself been recently blurring the natural moral conflicts that appear in the tissue of the text and pushing them backstage? I shall try to sum up several explanations that arise from Booth's book and some of my own thoughts.

The first explanation springs from the strengthening and deepening knowledge of psychology, which makes it possible to understand better the sources of failings and discrepancies in human behavior, an understanding that causes us to reduce greatly the strength of our moral and overall judgment. To understand, ergo to forgive, so said the poet. Indeed, the more sophisticated our psychological understanding, the more difficult it is for us to connect to the simple and obvious moral judgment required of us with regard to a character such as Shakespeare's Iago or Molière's Tartuffe or Dickens's Fagin or Pecksniff. Until the end of the nineteenth century, it was possible to present, whether through psychological naïveté or psychological principal, an evil and corrupt person or a pure and good person as a firm factor within the human situation described in a piece of literature. Today, it seems as though it is less easy for the serious modern novelist to present a major character whose good or bad traits are a "given" element that is thrown into the story without any extra explanations. In our current awareness, there is no such thing as a person who is simply bad or good. Such a person is disturbed, deprived of love, paranoid, frustrated, filled with all sorts of complexes inher-

ited by his or her parents or surroundings. On the other hand, a
pleasant and good character in a novel cannot be accepted at face
value without causing us to suspect that the goodness and charity
that character reflects are no more than responses to hidden and
crooked impulses, whose mantle of righteousness can be pulled aside
to allow them to cause damage to their environment.

Marceaux, hero of Camus's *The Stranger* (a novella of such importance that I believe it opened the era of modern literature following
the Second World War), who, for no reason, shoots an Arab on the
beach in Algeria, cannot be seen as a bad person according to the
new concept. He is "alienated" or "shallow"; he does not understand
the ways of the world. It is modernism that is guilty of his crime. In
other cases, novelists will rake up childhood hardships in order to
understand the moral misformations of the soul. Society, economic
conditions, parent-child relations are placed on trial as powerful
partners to the character's evil deeds.

In his novel *Crime and Punishment*, Dostoyevsky omitted many details about Raskolnikov's childhood, made little of his having lost his
father as a child, and did not develop a real elaboration on his relationship with his mother and sister. He made these choices, I believe, so that psychology (Dostoyevsky had a deep knowledge and
sensitive attitude to psychology) would not attract our attention
away from the moral dilemma that stands at the novel's center: Does
an individual have the right for self-fulfillment via the murder of a
"human flea"? A murder of this kind is no longer possible in a modern-day novel because psychology would not let him remain within
the simplicity of his own moral dilemma. Other murderers in Dostoyevsky's later novels, such as Rogozhin in *The Idiot* and Smardiakov
in *The Brothers Karamazov*, are wrapped in a psychological blanket that
is stronger than Raskolnikov's.

Of course, I do not think that in the end the psychological explanations dispel all the moral dilemmas awakened by the text, but they

do dull the immediate sharpness of these dilemmas and force us to hone and vary our definitions of moral judgment to those areas "covered" by psychology. Perhaps they even make us do the opposite—introduce the chisel of moral judgment into the character's subconscious, as we shall try to do later in the discussion on the story "A Rose for Emily" and on the novel *In the Prime of Her Life*.

The second reason for the withdrawal of moral judgment from literary criticism springs from the growth of legal influence in our lives, which is gradually overshadowing moral debate. More and more we tend to see the world through legal rather than ethical spectacles. Because we live in a democratic society, in which we are supposed to have faith in our system of lawmaking, we are used to the fact that the place in which to settle disputes regarding good or bad is the courthouse, where sharp-tongued lawyers are able sometimes to prove that a murderer is not exactly a murderer, but something else. We identify what is good in accordance with what the law allows us and what is bad in accordance with what the law forbids us. If we are allowed to drive one hundred miles per hour, it must be good, even if it creates a clear danger to human life. Sexual harassment is what the law defines as sexual harassment, which frees us from the need to take a personal stance that defines the act as good or bad and leaves the decision to the law. And because we feel that the legal system is constantly increasing its boundaries and becoming more liberal and advanced, we are quite content to let it do our "moral work" for us.

The third reason, I believe, is tied to the amazing development over recent years of the media in all its aspects, which also deals—admittedly on a superficial level—with moral issues, but also with speed, with efficiency, and with perseverance, both on social and personal levels. Literature often seems to be preceded by the media in penetrating certain new moral issues—for example, those concerning medicine or the status of women or homosexuality—because the media has a way of connecting quickly and immediately to the demands of political correctness, which is basically led by moral sensitivities that demand more equality between various sectors of society and atonement for old injustices. The widespread exposure enjoyed by the media makes its "moral work" both popular and immediate, and it seems to literature that nothing is left but to save its honor and hide away in its own little neurotic corner and try to pluck out yet another undiscovered psychological nuance or two—or to bemoan the superficiality of modern life. Indeed, there is something ironic about the fact that in keeping with the demands of political correctness, current literary editors (especially American ones) diligently weed out the "moral ineptitude" and the literary slips of the tongue that spring from a shortage of sensitivity and that are sprinkled liberally in modern short stories and novels. In other words, not only is it of no use to expect the writers to lead and invent the new sensitivities, but it is necessary to check them and to make sure they do not stumble over the "mistakes" of the past.

The fourth reason relates to the concept that art is judged mainly according to its shape and the rules it determines for itself with regard to what is aesthetic. Any discussion on the issue of morals, therefore, not only misses the real debate that can and must be held about literature, but also lays down unnecessary and misleading assumptions with regard to human characters whose personalities and actions can be studied according to former literary moral criteria.

The fifth reason is based on the fear that any moral discussion, especially during our own century, with its clear and definite ideological character, might sneak in a kind of ideological censorship—whether religious or otherwise—that would take the side either of the writer or of the reader. Such censorship would occur not necessarily in countries under totalitarian communist or fascist government, but in countries that enjoy democratic freedom of the kind that is constantly subjected to stormy ideological debates such as the one surrounding socialism.

Just a few months ago, I told one of my colleagues about writing this book, and I immediately sensed that he suspected me of trying to weave morality into literature. For a reader to use moral judgment with regard to the behavior of characters in a book seemed to my colleague to be at best irrelevant and at worst dangerous. He suspected me of trying to evaluate works of literature according to a scale of moral values that are outside of literature. My colleague is more or less my age, but he maintains a youthful spirit and is faithful to the literary awareness of our generation, formed during the 1950s. When we started to write, we felt a need to separate ourselves from the generation of writers and poets that preceded us, the War of Independence generation, whose writing was, to our taste, too strictly stamped with ideology and morality. Those writers and poets intensely experienced the War of Independence and with a blend of fresh nationalism and leftist socialism used their work to try to come to terms with different moral values. One of the outstanding works written by that generation is S. Yizhar's *The Prisoner,* which served as a model in many a stormy debate in schools and youth movements. The book's hero, the anonymous soldier, was subject time after time to a public tribunal, with young advocates or prosecutors standing up to accuse or defend him.

Our feeling was that moral debates prevented literature from taking wing and flying, and created in the reader inhibitions that stopped him or her from opening up to the deeper experiences that cannot and should not be judged merely according to their moral value. This concept—which leaned on the literary atmosphere in the world at that time, especially the existentialism wafting in from Europe and reaching even the Middle East—encouraged us all to write stories whose ideological and moral aspect made way for the psychological or form-aesthetic aspect. But I believe that now, when this particular "revolt" is long over and everyone is talking about the "death of ideologies," it is possible to take a new and more relaxed look at the moral debates of the past.

Anyway—and this allegation might be the harshest against moral discussions in literature—can there be objective criteria according to which a serious debate can be conducted on this issue at this of all times, when literary criticism is doing its best to adopt clear and accurate tools for research? After all, what a writer sees as moral or immoral—or even amoral—in this or that behavior of the characters he created is not necessarily obvious to his or her readers. It is especially difficult to reach a consensus among readers on one or other moral judgment when we tend more and more to assume (and respect) the multiplicity of cultural—and moral—codes in human society.

When literary criticism involves itself with the analysis of philology or the form and structure of a text or even the psychological motives of the characters, it appeals first and foremost to the reader's comprehension and relies on an understanding resulting from a mutual reading of the text. But the moment it begins dealing with moral evaluation, it finds itself entering the scope of extremely relative issues that must take into consideration all the various moral shades in each individual reader's stance because a moral stance is, in the final analysis, a personal stance. And because these various fine shades are what interest us in a literary text, an agreed upon, accepted debate and certainly any moral judgment and evaluation become difficult and complex.

I have only one reply to all these assertions, which is, to me at least, also quite convincing: whether we like it or not, every artistic work that deals with human relations has in it a moral aspect because all human relationships may be evaluated according to moral categories. Even a book of commentaries such as this one includes a moral situation between me and my reader, who examines my words not only according to the criteria of originality, knowledge, and intelligence, but also in accordance with moral criteria. For example, do I make a point of quoting accurately ideas borrowed from others? Or am I concealing my sources? Am I "bending" the meaning of a text to make it conform to my conclusions, or am I being fair in my interpretation? On what moral values do I base my moral preferences in making my interpretations? And so on.

The existence of a moral aspect in every piece of prose is what caused Jean-Paul Sartre to define the essential difference between prose (and in this case, theater also) and the other arts (including poetry) in his well-known book *Literature, What?* In all the other arts, no significant regard is given to issues of morality in the form and artistic content of a work, whereas in prose, theater, and cinema there exists a moral regard in the mere fact of presenting the relationships between characters.

Morality is not some far-off shining star suspended in the sky of our lives. It is omnipresent; it can be found everywhere that human beings are conducting interpersonal relationships, from the small cell that constitutes a marriage or family, to an individual's society, to his nation, and even to the international community. It may be that the commentator on a certain work of literature will find that its author or one of his or her heroes makes no reference whatsoever to questions of ethics that are demanded by certain situations. The reader, however, is entitled to relate to this lack and to try to learn from it about the quality and intentions of the novel's heroes. Even the black holes left behind by the novel, those things that remain unsaid and undone, are an integral part of it, and their effect on the reading is part of the creative activity.

The withdrawal of literature from the scope of large-scale moral debate is not good either for literature or for morality because no matter how professionally successful the work of the media and the importance of the courts of law, they are not as capable of bringing a person to so deep a level of empathy as is literature. Supposing, for example, that instead of the wonderful book by Harriet Beecher Stowe, *Uncle Tom's Cabin*—which was published in 1852 and aroused such deep and active empathy among people in the northern United States, turning into a powerful myth throughout the country and

prompting so many to join the struggle for the abolition of slavery—
a TV crew had been sent to Uncle Tom's cabin to interview the slave
and, to maintain a balance, his owners as well. I doubt if, under such
circumstances, the spiritual and perhaps political results would have
been the same.

There is a significant difference between the way in which literature creates the moral catharsis and the activity of the media. Literature does not expect its devotees to understand, but to identify. The
power of this identification lies in the fact that the moral issue does
not remain on the cognitive level, but becomes part of the reader's
personality and independence, his or her own personal problem.
Thus, the moral touch, if it succeeds, shocks the deeper strata of the
individual's soul.

Plato feared the effect of the negative morality of poets and believed that they and their poetry had to be checked very carefully
before being given a place in his ideal state. In his old age, Tolstoy
spoke out against a certain kind of literature, including his own great
novels, because he was concerned about their amoral effect on society. The two shared a common belief that art, especially literature,
has a powerful spiritual influence and a clear moral affinity.

Nowadays such theories would be received with a smile of deri-
sion. Nowadays, the attitude to art and literature is not so serious
and concerned, and no such heavy responsibility is heaped upon
them.

About seventy years ago in a Paris concert hall, an angry audience
threw rotten eggs at the performers of Stravinsky's ballet *The Rite of
Spring* because they saw in this music a coarse provocation against all
their values, not only musical but also moral. Who would take the
trouble today of protesting in the name of values of any kind—even
uttering a polite cry—against a modernistic piece of music or a new
book? At most, there would be lack of interest, a shrug of the shoulder, or weak applause, a fear that this composition might in time turn

out to be a new version of *The Rite of Spring*. In the world of entertain-
ment, everything goes, and the only question is whether it was a success or not. That is why no one expects literature to deliver any "new
tidings," rather merely an "experience."

In writing this book, I am fulfilling a modest mission—to arouse renewed interest in the moral and ethical aspects of the written text.
Because I do not consider myself to be a researcher of literature—
certainly not one who has anything new to say on the theory of literary criticism, rather merely one who comments on works of
literature—most of this book consists of discussions of nine literary
works. The fact that I am a writer myself makes it possible, or at least
so it seems to me, to focus more closely on the "kitchen work" of the
literary creation and in so doing to discover sometimes not only the
options an author chose, but also those that he or she deliberately
overlooked.

I chose to look at nine works here, both early classics and pieces
from the twentieth century, stories from Hebrew literature and from
the literature of the world. I do not know if I shall succeed in uncov-
ering new faces in such well-known texts, which have already been
intensively reviewed, but if I do, it will be just one more proof of the
powerful ability of the "moral issue" to illuminate the text in a different light.

All that remains, therefore, is to clarify what questions the
book deals with and the criteria I used to choose the works I discuss
here.

The general question relative to all the works is whether it is possible for a discussion that focuses mainly on the moral issues pertain-
ing to the interpersonal relationships in a given text to present us
with new understandings and sensitivities that we could not have
reached within other discussions. Some years ago, in a course I gave
at the University of Haifa, I tried to examine the role played by the

plot in various novels. It became apparent to me that some difficulties and misunderstandings in works such as Tolstoy's *Anna Karenina* or Agnon's *A Simple Story* were clarified by means of a thorough examination of specific questions relating to the plot, such as how a crisis was solved or the way in which the book came to its end—for example, the decisive reason for Anna Karenina's suicide or the way in which Herschel extricates himself from his problems and achieves a harmonious relationship with his wife.

For the first part of the book, I chose three works—the biblical tale of Cain and Abel, the drama *Alcestis* by Euripides, and the story "The Guest" by Albert Camus. Through them I try to show how clear-cut rhetorical elements in the fiber of the story—such as language, rhythm, distance of the storyteller from the story, choice of details, ways of stressing these details, and the order in which they are presented—have the power to act on the reader in such a way as to cause him to identify and even agree with moral positions and behavior that, had they been presented to him directly, from without the story, would possibly have turned him off altogether. We are familiar with the power of literary suggestion from various aspects of a reader's reaction, mental shock, and empathy with elements that are emotionally alien to him, but is it also in the power of literature to undermine the reader's clearly defined moral position and to put to sleep his natural moral opposition?

I picked three works, Brenner's "The Way Out" and *Nerves*, and Dostoyevsky's *The Eternal Husband*, to examine that complex region of relationships between morality and psychology to which I alluded at the beginning of this introduction.

I chose two works, Faulkner's "A Rose for Emily" and Agnon's *In the Prime of Her Life*, to examine the moral responsibility that can be attached to the act of pushing things into the subconscious. This is an important question, one that is on the threshold of moral debate, but one, I believe, that literature has the ability to clearly substantiate.

And I chose the final work—the modern, almost postmodern,

story "Cathedral" by the excellent American writer Raymond Carver in order to discuss the old question of whether the moral development of a character in a literary work can increase its aesthetic power.

Many people believe that because truth and goodness are intertwined, we are doing a good thing by exposing truth; and literature that is trying to expose more truth about humanity, society, and the world—be it psychological, sociological, political, or even linguistic truth—is in any case fulfilling a moral objective. This belief, of course, has a certain truth, but it is not sufficient, not only because truth is an evasive, personal, partial, and often controversial entity in the regions in which literature is active, but also because although truth alone might help to distinguish between good and bad, it does not have in it the ability to reveal the difference and the moral determination. For this, special effort and attention are needed. Indeed, literature can touch and focus not only on reality, but also on the region of moral determination. This region is a true and natural grazing ground for literature and one that should not be relinquished. A metaphor I like to use is that readers, like explorers, draw and redraw a moral map as they read, and this moral map emerges from the rhetoric of the story.

This book is based on a course I gave in several universities in Israel and abroad, titled "The Moral Connection of Literary Text," so that between the written lines one can still define traces of the didactic tone of a lecture, together with the discourse and polemic of a teacher. The contribution of the many students who participated in this course is hidden between the lines, and it is to them that I dedicate the book, with thanks.

I also thank my wife and the many friends who read the manuscript and made extremely useful remarks. And I am grateful to Bernard Horn for his great help in revising the English version of this book.

Haifa 1998   Abraham B. Yehoshua

PART ONE

Moral Diversions Using the Text's Aesthetic Structure

Although I am dealing here with three separate texts, each significantly different from the others, I would like to use a discussion of them to illustrate how various kinds of literary rhetoric try to direct readers, and perhaps even succeed, leading and influencing them morally to a place it is most uncertain they could have reached or would have wanted to reach in an open and direct debate. In other words, the hidden power of the text can be found not only in its suggestive sympathy with emotional experience, but also in its out-of-sight push toward changing firm moral positions.

෴ 1 ෴

What Was the Real Punishment
Inflicted on History's First Murderer?

THE BIBLICAL STORY OF CAIN AND ABEL,
GENESIS 4

And the man knew Eve, his wife; and she conceived and bore Cain saying, I have acquired a manchild from the Lord. And she bore again, his brother Abel. And Abel was a keeper of sheep, but Cain was a tiller of the ground. And in the process of time it came to pass, that Cain brought of the fruit of the ground an offering to the Lord. And Abel, he also brought of the firstlings of his flock and of the fat parts thereof; but to Cain and to his offering he had not respect. And Cain was very angry and his face fell. And the Lord said to Cain, Why art thou angry? And why art thou crestfallen? If thou doest well, shalt thou not be accepted? And if thou doest not well, sin crouches at the door, and to thee shall be his desire. Yet thou mayest rule over him. And Cain talked with Abel his brother and it came to pass, when they were in the field, that Cain rose up against his brother Abel and slew him. And the Lord said to Cain, Where is Abel thy brother? And he said, I know not, am I my brother's keeper? And he said, What hast thou done? The voice of thy brother's blood cries to me from the ground. And now cursed art thou from the earth, which has opened her mouth to receive thy brother's blood from thy hand; when thou tillest the ground, it shall not henceforth yield to thee her strength; a fugitive and a vagabond shalt thou be on the earth. And Cain said to the Lord, My punishment is greater than I can bear. Behold, thou hast driven me out this day from the face of the earth; and it shall come to pass, that anyone that finds me shall slay me. And the Lord said to him, Therefore whoever slays Cain, vengeance shall be taken on him sevenfold. And the Lord set a mark upon Cain, lest any finding him should smite him. And Cain went out from the presence of the Lord and dwelt in the land of Nod, to the east of Eden. And Cain knew his wife; and she conceived and bore Hanokh and he built a city, and called the name of the city, after the name of his son, Hanokh.

We are told at the end of this story what happened to history's first murderer, according to the Bible. Following an exchange of harsh words with God, who places a curse on the murderer and forces a nomadic existence on him, Cain has the audacity to ask to be protected against any adversary who might want to kill him—whether in retribution for the murder of Abel or as a result of the increased vulnerability of the nomadic lifestyle God imposes on him (the text is unclear on this point). Indeed, God accedes to the murderer by stamping him with a sign, which will warn off any potential attacker, and in order to make this sign effective and clear to all, the Maker issues a warning of the serious consequence to be suffered by anyone who dares lay a finger on history's first murderer.

Fully armed against any eventual harm or revenge, Cain leaves the presence of God, but not to take up a harsh nomadic existence, detached from human society, as decreed by God. What he does is make his way to a new settlement in a place that is not far from the Garden of Eden and is known as the Land of Nod. Is the Land of Nod the right place for implementing the punishment of nomadism? Not necessarily. The Land of Nod is connected to nomadism only in that the Hebrew word for nomad is *navad* or "noded." Actually, according to the biblical text, Cain successfully undertakes the life of a settler. Not only does Cain's wife (did she exist before the murder?) give birth to a son, but from then on, he has no desire to eke out a livelihood by working the land, and quite rightly so, for after God curses the land for being partner to the murder of his brother, it becomes hard and rebellious, and makes life difficult for anyone trying to grow his daily bread out of it. Cain undergoes a "modern" transition from a rural to an urban lifestyle (the exact opposite of what is considered the life of a nomad), and the new town he builds and inaugurates is indeed his new home in all senses, if the name he gives it is the same as that of his son, Hanokh.[1]

When we go back to make a close and perfectly lucid study of the closing chapter of the story of Cain and Abel, as it is presented in the Bible, we are thus surprised to learn that not only does the murderer avoid severe punishment for his crime, but even the less severe punishment decreed for him by God is not carried out in the end. Thus, the murderer does not even return to the situation he was in prior to the murder, and a close study of the text shows us that his situation has even *improved*. But the second surprise is that the story's author has actually managed to deceive us. Not because he does not present all the facts—on the contrary, there is something cruelly honest in the biblical report of Cain's happy end—but in the way in which he anesthetizes and dims our natural sense of justice. Indeed, the story

1. This is the place to point out something preliminary and fundamental about how textual commentary is made in this book, especially with regard to biblical texts and to Greek drama. I attempt to make such commentary from within a direct examination of the texts themselves, without considering the abundance of historical, philological, or cultural commentary already available on them. I am not taking this approach through disregard or disdain for previous commentaries, but rather from a fundamental position that places the classical quality of these texts as a basic position. Their classicism is expressed in the fact that we are able to read them from beyond the conditions of their times with its their different moral and cultural values. Anyone who reads the Bible as a literary text that has special virtues or as a religious text with a profound spiritual meaning wishes to see it as text that is alive, that has value—notwithstanding its age—relevant to the reader. Thus, a preliminary reading is one that is textually direct, with a need for historical or philological commentary only in places that are really blocked.

of Cain and Abel is not saved forever in our awareness as a terrible miscarriage of justice on the part of God, who is a hero and partner in the story. The story does not cause us to come out in protest and to say, "If this is the way that Genesis begins, with the story of a cruel murder and such a happy ending for the murderer, not only is it no wonder that our world has been so full of murder stories ever since, but the question is, If this is the level of God's justice, should we be willing to accept his moral control of the world?

On the other hand, if we were to ask people who read about Cain and Abel in their youth what they remember of the story and what happened to Cain, many might remember that Cain did not pay with his life for the murder he committed. Most of them would describe him as a wild animal, alone and neglected in some remote cave, rejected by human society, suffering and persecuted, with the sign of God stamped like an ugly horn on his forehead, signaling more than a warning to potential assailants, but the disgrace of the murder.

In order to live in peace with this story, we have been obliged to balance the biblical picture in our moral imagination. But the question that has to be asked is: If the author of the story did indeed put to sleep our moral senses, what was his purpose in doing so? In other words, what is the *true* moral objective of this story?

We shall follow the story, paragraph by paragraph. "And the man knew Eve his wife." This is the first time in the Bible that the act of copulation between a man and a woman is described with a nice word, *knew*, a word that has in it something spiritual and noble—knowledge as a challenge of love, for the purpose of giving birth. The wife is the mysterious text that needs to be deciphered, and the man deciphers her through the act of love. Although, according to this description, the active initiative is the man's, the woman's material passivity is explained in the wealth and the mystery imbedded in her.

"And she conceived and bore Cain, saying, I have acquired a man-child from the Lord." Indeed, Cain was born as a result of this act of knowing love, and the author attaches great significance to the name given to the child by his mother—from the Hebrew word *kin* or "acquire." His birth took place with the help of God, and through it the mother has a renewed connection to God, acquisition being tantamount to ownership. In any case, the entire story of Cain's birth and naming bears witness to a great sense of respect on the part of the author for Cain and his status.

This status is reinforced when it comes to describing the birth of Abel, which is almost the exact opposite of that of Cain. "And she again bore, his brother Abel." Abel seems to have been born of Eve alone, without the need for Adam's *knowledge* of her. Not only does his name have no significance, but it has an almost cruel antisignificance—*hevel*, the Hebrew word for "nonsense," that which is meaningless. From the beginning, the only significance for Abel's existence lies in his being Cain's brother. Right from the start, the author singles out the main hero of this story, the one whose task it is to shoulder the drama—Cain.

From here on, Adam and Eve disappear from the story, and their disappearance is extremely significant from the point of view of the author's moral interests. Their presence or any mention of them would have certainly made it difficult for the author to lead the story in the way in which he intends.

"And Abel was a keeper of sheep, but Cain was a tiller of the ground. And in the process of time, it came to pass, that Cain brought of the fruit of the ground an offering to the Lord. And Abel, he also brought of the firstlings of his flock and of the fat parts thereof." These new neutral facts with regard to the significance of the text give no indication as to a moral preference for one occupation over the other. Is there any special meaning to the fact that Abel is mentioned first? I think there is, if we expect that the firstborn son

should be mentioned before his younger brother. The change in order creates in us a certain sensitivity with regard to the sequence in
which things related to the brothers are presented. Thus, when one
line down, it says that Cain was the first to bring his offering to the
Lord, we do not conceive of this statement as merely a routine tech-
nicality that presents the seniority of the firstborn over his younger
brother. If the order was changed in the first sentence, then this is
not a case of mechanical but of palpable order. Cain is the first to
bring an offering to the Lord. In other words, the initiative for prof-
fering the offering is Cain's; Abel merely follows on.

Here stands the anchor that many readers grasp in order to give a
moral rationale to the story and especially to justify the question of
why God had respect for Abel's offering and no respect for Cain's.
Abel brought of the firstlings of his flock and of the fat parts thereof,
whereas Cain brought *only* of the fruit of the ground—as if Abel had
brought choicer examples of his efforts and Cain's offerings were
more mundane. As far as I am concerned, there is no foundation for
this hypothesis. Abel did indeed bring the firstlings as an offering,
but is the cause of Cain's downfall that he did not bring his firstlings,
of which no mention is made? True, although there is a symbolic
value to the offering of firstlings, this significance is not acute. Is it
possible that for so trivial a fact the Lord would make so harsh a dis-
crimination between the two brothers that would ultimately result in
murder?

I reject this notion for the simple reason that the Lord does not
explain his nonacceptance of Cain's offering as being because Cain
did not bring firstlings, but for a much more substantial and serious
reason. If that had been the reason for the Lord's preference of Abel's
offering, Cain could have easily remedied the matter and achieved
the Lord's approval. I believe that as soon as the reader reaches the
moment in which Abel's offering is accepted and Cain's is rejected,
and it says in the Bible, "And Cain was very angry and his face fell,"

it is quite easy to understand the pain and insult he is suffering from the rejection of his offering.

God is very important to Cain, who is the first to make his offering and who is deeply angered and insulted by God's rejection of the offering. Thus, God's questions—"Why art thou angry? And why art thou crestfallen?"—appear to be rhetorical, superficial, and superfluous. But it seems that they are not from God's point of view, who believes that Cain should have understood the reason for the rejection of his offering. The Lord respects the way in which Cain's self-awareness cannot only understand the reason for the rejection, but also justify it.

And here comes the key sentence in the text, which is complex and difficult, but also full of profound meaning: "If thou doest well, shalt thou not be accepted? And if thou doest not well, sin crouches at the door, and to thee shall be his desire." A possible explanation is: if you do well, you will enjoy an advantage; if you do not do well, you will be stricken by sin, and although sin is drawn to you, you are still able to control it.

In essence, Cain is substantially inferior from a moral point of view not because of any sinful acts he has committed, but because his thoughts and his drives are drawn to sin. He is a man who is *destined to sin*, although he has the ability and the strength to overcome the evil within him. A gift from a person who implicitly has bad and criminal thoughts in his heart is seen by the Lord as an act of falsehood and is rejected. When the heart is impure, it is not possible to legitimize an external ritual of gift giving. What could Cain have done, then? In actual fact, nothing. No allegation is made of a specific sin that Cain committed (in which case, the Lord could have admonished him), rather only of thoughts and ugly intentions. Abel symbolizes here a person who is pure of mind and has no sinful tendencies, perhaps through lack of imagination or perhaps because of a simple and uncomplicated mental structure. In any case, God's statement can be summed up thus: "Although you are two brothers, in fact you are not equal in my eyes, not because of anything you have done but because of what is inside of you."

The arena here is an internal one. The debate is on something internal—on a moral feeling about potential thoughts and eventualities—and not on concrete situations. Although the world is not yet demanding moral decisions in clear human situations, the moral context exists in the fact of the internal moral attitude to it. Good and bad stand beyond action. Cain is disqualified (not punished!) not for what he did, but for what is happening within him.

This concept is serious and harsh. It is easier to avoid committing a sin than it is to refrain from sinful thoughts. Cain feels a stinging pain because the blessing that is withheld from himself is given so freely to his brother, so it is quite natural that after his conversation with God, he turns first and foremost to his brother Abel, whether to be helped by him or to do away with him.

"And Cain talked with Abel his brother." Something seems to be lacking in this part of the text. I say *seems* because in this debate we are relating to the biblical text not as some ancient archaeological text, but as a purely literary text. The fact that the author does not go into detail over the words spoken by Cain to Abel might indicate a weak and unclear attempt at dialogue, an attempt that by its mere content is destined to fail because how can Abel explain to his brother his own pure and natural quality?

"And Cain rose up against Abel his brother and slew him." Abel does not respond to Cain, and, gripped with the power of jealousy, Cain kills Abel, his brother. Because Cain is unable to be what the Lord asks of him, he wants to destroy the criterion according to which he is being judged. Is the fact that the word *brother* is constantly repeated beneficial to the murderer or not? I venture to believe that in the end it is to the murderer's benefit. In murdering his brother, he is also murdering something of himself. I admit that this issue is debatable and that opinions differ as to crimes committed within a family framework. There are those who would tend to be very severe in judging such crimes in the belief that a crime committed against family members, who had faith in their relative, is worthy of the worst kind of punishment. On the other hand, there are also those who would try to find a mitigating side to such crimes. It might be assumed that anyone who has reached a state whereby he can harm a person dear to him—his parents, children, spouse, or another family member—and thereby harms himself also must have had good reason for doing so (extenuating, sometimes), such as troubled personal interaction with them. An attack on a total stranger, on the other hand, always gives the impression of being more severe and more cruel because it is apparently more thoughtless and mercenary.

Attention should be paid to the fact that the Bible gives no description of the murder itself. There is no description of the murderer's feelings or of his parents' reaction to the act. The only words that echo from the description of this murder are *rose up, brother, slew.*

"And the Lord said to Cain, Where is Abel thy brother? And he said, I know not: am I my brother's keeper?" It is at this moment that our revulsion for Cain is at its peak, more even than at the moment of the murder itself, which we conceive as being more tragic than vile because we are still under the hold of the desperation that brought Cain to committing the murder, the criterion that determines his inferiority. But the moment he tries to *deny* the murder is the moment when we feel the full measure of revulsion toward the murderer. It is clear that God knows where the murdered man's body is laid, but he wants to prove to Cain the depth of the lie that he is living, and through his rhetorical question, God reveals the weight of the lie.

Using his literary means, the author creates not simply a story about a disagreement between two brothers, but a dramatic dialogue between a man called Cain and the Lord his God. Abel is no more than a completely sufferable tool in this dialogue, so that in himself he is not important; he is *hevel* (in Hebrew, "air, mist"). His death is less central than Cain's lie to God, so much so that right from the beginning God is indifferent to the murder, and his only intention is to prove to Cain his criminal tendencies, which are completely unworthy of the grace of God—to prove the justice of his first assessment of Cain's corrupt nature and by doing so to justify his refusal of Cain's offering.

Even the words "What hast thou done? The voice of thy brother's blood cries to me from the earth" refer to more than the actual murder. They aim at proving that nothing is lost to the eye of the Lord or that the attempt at lying has failed because God can hear the call of blood from within the earth.

Thus, it is clear that the right punishment in this particular context is not the execution of the murderer because revenge for the murder is not what is necessary in the dialogue that this story spreads before us, but rather the absolute and total discontinuation of contact with the Lord and the loss of his grace. "And from thy face I shall be hid," says Cain in shame. The punishment of nomadism is seen, therefore, as a constant escape from the Lord, as a lack of inner equilibrium rather than true wandering. Thus, the happy ending, as it appears at first sight, is misleading. As soon as Cain's equilibrium is shaken, from the moment a feeling of unrest is planted within him, he is in a state of constant flight from the Lord; building the town, producing a son, these are only the outer peelings of the Lord's presence from which Cain shall hide.

I am trying to lead my commentary in this direction because otherwise it is impossible for us to reconcile ourselves to Cain's "happy ending," which should have aroused in us a powerful feeling of disgust, both toward the biblical storyteller, who finds it fitting to tell us so immoral a tale, and toward the Lord, who finds himself partner to a story that is so problematic.

But let's imagine to ourselves that the story of Cain and Abel was written differently, without making any factual change in the original text:

> And the man knew Eve his wife, and she conceived and bore Cain, saying, I have acquired a manchild from the Lord. And the man knew his wife Eve, and she conceived and bore Abel and said, Even the air from his mouth is dear to my heart. Abel was a tender of sheep and Cain a tiller of the land. And it came to pass that Cain brought of the fruit of the earth an offering to God, and Abel brought also of the firstlings of his flock and of their milk. And the Lord had respected Abel and his offering, and he rejected Cain's offering. And Cain was very angry. And the Lord said to Cain, Why are you angry and why are you crestfallen? If you do well, shall you not be accepted? And if you do not well, sin crouches at the door and to thee shall be his desire. And Cain talked to Abel his brother. Let us go for a walk in the breeze of the day. And while they were in the field, Cain rose up against Abel his brother. And Abel begged for his life, and Cain did not listen to his brother's pleading, but thrust the knife into his throat.
>
> And Adam and Eve heard of the murder and hurried to the field and saw Abel their son lying in a pool of blood, and they rent their clothes and cried bitter tears and laid a terrible curse on Cain. And the Lord said to Cain: Where is Abel your brother? And he said I know not, am I my brother's keeper?

This "new" text contains no fact that contradicts the original text, and all the additions are perfectly feasible with regard to what was written in the original text. Only an elaboration on the point of view—the description of the murder, the parents' reaction, the previous value that was given to Abel's name—and this elaboration makes it difficult for the reader to reconcile himself to the story's other ending, the so-called "happy ending." Employing new literary means, moving aside the focal point, elaborating on the story—all these techniques cause a shake-up in the moral map, yet they are based on the very same facts.

The question is, What went to work on our moral feelers, which were supposed to have reacted differently to the injustice of Cain's light sentence? In that same book of Genesis, five chapters after the story of Cain and Abel, and after the Noah's Ark affair, there comes a moral rule that is completely different with regard to punishment due to any murderer: "Whoso sheds a man's blood by man shall his blood be shed: for in the image of God made he man." This is a social law of the first order, according to which human society protects itself against the acts of injustices and evil that take place within it. But in the story of Cain and Abel, this firm moral code is not implemented; rather another set of moral sensitivities is presented, one that is more complex and therefore also more profound and richer, but also more problematic. In this set of sensitivities, God is given a more important active role than the "in the image of" that serves as a uniform standard after the flood. God is a partner in the profound discourse with man on his inner self, on the truth and the lie that is within him, on his thoughts and on his potential for evil and his ability to overcome it. Thus, Abel, who is murdered in the course of this story, does not turn into a victim that demands immediate vengeance worthy of murder; rather, he is only one component of this complicated discourse.

According to the story of Cain and Abel, from the very beginning, human beings are not equal to each other in the sight of God because their inner selves—whether as a result of congenital traits, their destiny, or their education or consequences—are individual, differing from one person to the next. People are not judged merely on their actions, but also on what is inside their souls, their thoughts, and their personalities because all these elements are important in motivating their actions. God takes the responsibility for the significant difference between one person and the other. He does not content himself with the uniform "image" of God with which he stamps every person; he also deals with the various qualities ingrained in people. Thus, just as God will refuse to accept an offering from a man whose inner self is bad, so too he cannot judge this man too harshly for having committed a murder that resulted from this very rejection. God is responsible for his rejection, which makes him circumspectly responsible for the murder committed as a result of the rejection, giving us the reason for the light punishment.

The line that differentiates substantially between two people in accordance with the moral weight of their inner selves is developed and preserved throughout the Bible (alongside and in contradiction to other lines). Moreover, its strength will be stressed specifically because it is tested—as in the story of Cain and Abel—in the midst of biological families, between siblings and other relationships (Cain and Abel, Abraham and Lot, Isaac and Ishmael, Jacob and Esau, Joseph and his brothers, Israel and the other nations, and so on). I believe, in the end, that this line is tragic and problematic, constantly arousing contention. Against this line comes another one, a more open and democratic one, by which a person's moral rights and obligations are be examined in accordance with the simple and all-powerful criterion of the "image"—"Whoso sheds a man's blood by man shall his blood be shed: for in the image of God made he man." There is but *one* image, and the personality behind it is of no importance. The thoughts, the dilemmas, the inner selves—all these are not placed under any moral scrutiny, only the acts.

According to the "in the image" principle, I daresay that it would have been contingent upon God to accept Cain's offering; he would not have discriminated against him on the basis of his inner self. But, then, if Cain had committed murder, for any reason, he would have been executed immediately. God, who is cruelly selective before the murder and lenient with the punishment he metes out to the murderer, is a different God from the one about whom it is asked, "Shall not the Judge of all the earth do right?"

The thing that interests us in the story of Cain and Abel is the private moral correction made by many readers in their imagination in order to atone for God's miscarriage of justice in not inflicting any real punishment on Cain. Thus, a moral analysis, such as was made here, not only exposes the true substance of the story, but also explains why we were wrong about it.

✍ 2 ✍

The Morals of a Husband
Who Lets His Wife Die in His Place

ALCESTIS,

BY EURIPIDES

It is with supreme caution that I undertake a debate on the play *Alcestis* by Euripides. I read the translated text in all its simplicity as a reader who is facing a work of pure classicism, the value of which glows with the light of the centuries that have passed since it was written. I am making no attempt at analyzing the spirit of the times in which it was written. I have no intention of delving into the inner codes of Greek religion and society that are so deeply ingrained in Euripides' and in his readers' or listeners' cultural discourse. As a modern-day reader, I am looking for some kind of moral significance that would be relevant for me within the plot and with regard to the characters who emerge from the dialogues and monologues of the play. Only when the text appears to me to be blocked and unclear do I resort to the comments supplied by the experts and the translators. I am sure that I am missing out on entire layers of significance because of my lack of familiarity with classical codes. However, in my direct reading, which deals with the text's moral map, I dare to be audacious and say that I do not need these codes.

The Hebrew version of *Alcestis,* on which I base my commentary of the text, is the one by Aharon Shabtai, whose translations of Greek plays are in a language that is clear, simple, and juicy, proving time and again that true classics do not need to be shrouded in heavy, gold-trimmed cloaks in order to be classical. Also, I have been greatly assisted by the translator's enlightening comments in his introduction to the Hebrew version.

What, then, is the plot of this drama? For a drama it is, rather than a tragedy or a comedy.

Admetus, king of Pheres in northern Greece has to die. No special explanation is given in the drama as to why he has to die. No hint is made as to the crime he has committed, which he now has to pay for with his life. He is a relatively young man (his children are still small), and quite clearly it is not time for him leave the world. Zeus, the king of the gods, has exiled his son Apollo to Admetus's palace as punishment for killing the Cyclops. Admetus welcomes Apollo warmly and treats him with respect, and in return, Apollo makes a special arrangement with the Fates to allow someone else to be persuaded to die in place of Admetus when the time comes. Now is the time, and Admetus has no qualms about asking his aging parents to die in his place. But his mother and father are not overkeen to die instead of their son, nor are other members of his family, of whom he is not too ashamed to ask this rather novel favor. There is no knowing if, in desperation, Admetus appeals also to his wife, Alcestis, or whether she herself is so overcome with pity for her husband that she offers to die in place of the father of her children. Admetus accepts his wife's offer, and the drama, *Alcestis*, opens on the day Alcestis is due to be led to her death. It is a simple plot: Queen Alcestis is carried off to her death instead of her husband, but at the end of the same day, she is returned from Hades following the intervention of her husband's friend Heracles and reinstated in the arms of her ecstatic husband.

It is a stormy and turbulent day, full of conflicts and wild accusations, promises, and justification hurled from all sides with regard to the extraordinary event that is about to take place. The gods, Apollo, and Heracles also take an active part in the drama of Admetus and Alcestis, and, of course, don't let us forget the chorus, with its ongoing commentary challenging all those present.

We shall open, as we did with Cain and Abel, at the end of the story. Alcestis is raised back from Hades by Heracles and returned to her husband, Admetus. The king is not permitted to speak with his wife; for the next three days, she must remain speechless, consecrated to the gods of Hades. There is no doubt, however, that after those three days happiness will reign once again in the home of Admetus—this time, doubly so. In this final scene of the drama, Admetus takes his leave with the following words: "To all the citizens of my realm I ordain that dances be instituted for these happy events and that the altars be made to steam with atoning sacrifices of cattle. We have changed our state of life from its former condition for the better. *I shall not deny that I am fortunate.*"[1]

I am making a point of stressing "I shall not deny that I am fortunate" because I consider it to be a daring and outspoken thing to say by a man who, throughout the play, has constantly been under verbal attack, either direct or indirect, from all sides, including from his wife, who offered to die in his stead. When he finally achieves salvation, Admetus does not say, "Oh, how lucky I am," offering thanks to the gods and Heracles for their good graces. Rather, with all the arrogant confidence in the world, he announces that he "shall not deny that [he is] fortunate." In other words, not only does he have no misgivings as to his behavior, but he considers it to have been perfectly

---

1. Translator's note: The correct and accurate translation of the Greek verb *eutykahon,* with which the play comes to an end, is "I did it" or "I succeeded." It is not a passive but an active verb. The author's interpretation of the Greek drama is based on Aharon Shabtai's translation into Hebrew; the current translation quotes the English translation, with the less accurate and much less powerful "I shall not deny that I am fortunate."

correct and successful—a success that is both existential (because he and his wife are still alive at the end of the play) and *moral*.

Moreover, it would appear that the author, too, is party to Admetus's moral sanction of his behavior. Euripides deliberately supplies a happy ending to the play, meritorious to its two main heroes, and Alcestis's unexpected rescue from the gods of Hades at the end of the drama is an *integral* part of the events. This is no random occurrence, a kind of deus ex machina that happens at the end of many plays in order to help the playwright unravel some unsuccessful knots that he tied in the course of his play. Rather, Euripides appears to be trying to convince us that Admetus "earned" honorably the wonderful aid Heracles extends to him. Thus, as a good ending it is highly significant and not merely a technical good ending. In other words, were we to return Admetus and Alcestis to the starting point of the play, fully aware of all the trials and tribulations they are destined to suffer, but with no knowledge of the story's end, they would no doubt act in exactly the same way.

In this age of feminism, so outspoken a statement as Admetus gives in his closing speech, therefore, can be seen as quite repulsive and difficult to stomach. The husband either demands or raises no objection to his wife's dying in his stead, and we, the readers and lookers-on, are expected to view this state of affairs not as a strange fact, but as something that is morally correct—so much so that the gods actually condone it.

I have no way of knowing how, in the final analysis, each reader will face the moral conclusion determined by this drama. I have already pointed out in my introduction that more than the other elements that we define in a work of literature, the moral element depends on the individual reader's own personal moral values. But we can certainly delve deeply into the text in order to move across the moral map used by the playwright to lead us hand over fist to that same epilogue in which Admetus declares his fortune in words the playwright obviously chose to arouse not our revulsion, but rather our sympathy.

The play opens with a monologue by the god Apollo, who, although he is responsible for Admetus's trade-off with death, does not remain to witness the harsh results of his act, but leaves Admetus's palace so as not to become tainted by Alcestis's death. In this exit, he might be hinting that the gods can sometimes propose new and daring options to humans, but the responsibility for the decision humans make must remain their own. Death arrives at the palace prior to Apollo's departure, and the two enter a dialogue that ends in bitter hostility. The logic and wisdom of Death's words do not fall short of Apollo's pathos, and because Apollo has no real argument to persuade Death of the justice of the trade-off that he set up, he reveals to all of us the end of the drama that is about to unfold before us. He foresees a visit by Heracles, who will struggle with the gods of Hades and bring back Alcestis to her husband and children.

The question is, What does Euripides disclose about the end of the drama before the events of the play even begin? Why does he not take advantage of the tension of his audience's curiosity to know what is going to happen? I do not intend to go into the possible reasons for an author's or playwright's announcing in advance what will become of the characters and events in his or her work. The writer's intention is sometimes to draw the readers' attention to the *how* of the plot's development, rather than to *what* is happening in it because the how refers usually to the ordinary or real issues in life and not to its what. But I think in this case the author's intention was to modify the readers' instinctive aversion—not to mention revulsion—to the strange deal to which they made themselves party.

When we read books and watch movies that have the kind of dialogue that leads us to expect a happy ending, it is infinitely easier for us to cope with all the trials and tribulations that lie in store for the story's "good guys." And it is no different in this particular story.

Especially because the author is trying to create moral sympathy for the king and his actions, which appear to be morally dubious, he makes a point right at the beginning of promising the reader that Alcestis will be saved in the end. This early promise of a happy ending enables readers to modify their hostility somewhat and to be more attentive to Admetus's behavior and reasoning, especially in light of the sharp reprisals the king will be made to face in the course of the drama. Alcestis will be saved in the end. Why? How? These details we are yet to discover. Her salvation does not, of course, ensure any kind of sympathy for Admetus's behavior, but it does at least make it possible for the viewer to enjoy a certain relaxation in watching the drama unfold.

After Apollo leaves and Death enters the palace to collect his booty, the chorus appears. The chorus consists of a small group of people from the land of Pheres—a kind of Admetus fan club who have come to support their hero in his darkest hour. They do not represent society as a whole, only a part of it, as the Handmaid points out: "Not everyone is so well disposed to his lords as to stand by them in their troubles. But you have been friendly to my master from of old." In other words, there are no few subjects in the realm who are disgusted by their king's trade-off.

This support group is very instrumental in singling out and emphasizing the elements in the moral map being spread out by the play. Because the sympathy of these supporters—notwithstanding their hesitant tone—will be presented through clear-cut ideological conformity with regular and routine claims, it will stress the singularity of Admetus's personality and the special moral aspect of his behavior and values. Had this support group been of the kind that identified completely with Admetus, we would have felt Euripides was making things easy for himself by justifying Admetus's deeds. However, had the chorus been made up of a group of completely hostile opposition forces, Admetus's struggle against them would probably have worn him out, and he would have lost any chance of drawing sympathetic attention to the singularity with which his be-havior justifies—or rather defends—his problematic act. The inter-mediary position of a group that is reserved and hesitant in its support creates a good background for clarifying accurately the moral issue placed before us.

If we examine carefully the words of these devoted citizens, we can notice two elements being used to "smooth over the matter": first of all, the praise heaped on Alcestis, who sacrifices her own life, and second, King Admetus's appropriate behavior in organizing decent funeral arrangements and the kind of mourning ritual worthy of the rank of the deceased. The eulogy for Alcestis is twofold so that spe-cial dynamics are created with regard to the text's moral struggle to obtain the reader's sympathy for Admetus's act. (Once again, don't let us forget that this sympathy, ultimately, is the moral objective.) On the one hand, there is a swing principle in action here—the more we praise Alcestis, the more we protest against Admetus's selfish trade-off with death—but there is a conflicting principle at the same time. If Alcestis is willing to sacrifice her life for Admetus, maybe he's really worthy of it? It must be inconceivable, surely, that she is per-forming so noble an act of sacrifice for a man who is not moral, a man who is wicked and selfish.[2]

I am drawing a line that should add complexity to the moral map

2. If the readers of this drama wonder at the feasibility of such a trade-off with death, they should turn to other chapters in the history of the twentieth century, in which such deals were made possible—either during the Holocaust or in countries in which cruel, bloodthirsty dictatorships replaced the Greek option. Thus, the sit-uation described in this drama is not necessarily as far-fetched and unnatural as it would appear at first. Moreover, exchange-and-barter deals between people in gen-eral and between married couples in particular are carried out constantly on matters that are infinitely more important and serious, albeit less significant than the choice between life and death.

we are outlining here. When the chorus says, "Alcestis . . . has proven to us and to everyone that she is the noblest of wives," it is a statement that not only works against Admetus, but paradoxically also works in his favor. We shall check the development of this line later on.

In the meantime, the Admetus fan club requests that this whole unsavory business of trade-offs with death should be removed as soon as possible from the public agenda to erase the negative effect it has on society. They are wondering whether the death has already occurred and the burial and mourning rituals completed. The final sentence at this stage is quite typical: "All the rites have been accomplished by the king, upon the altars of all the gods do blood-dripping sacrifices abound. There is no remedy for these evils." The king who is responsible for all this evil becomes merely the one to have carried out what is necessary. And the trade-off is crowned here with the noncommittal term *evils*. So slimy and slippery are the tongues of politicians.

It is no wonder, therefore, that the Handmaid exits the palace into which Death has entered in all his glory and tries to put the ongoing tragedy back into its rightful proportions. A clearly critical tone is detected in her words, and because she is a handmaid who owes complete allegiance to her lord, this kind of rebuke is extremely daring and expresses real anger. The Handmaid refuses to lend a hand to the Admetus support group in their attempt at smoothing things over. She is not at all impressed by what the chorus has to say: "Let her [Alcestis] know that she dies glorious, the best woman under the sun by far." She retorts bitterly, "Certainly the best. Who would gainsay it? What must the woman be who would surpass her?" With greatest sensitivity, she describes the painful way in which Alcestis takes her leave of her family, her servants, her home. Obviously, these heartrending descriptions are aimed at shocking the Admetus support group, to make sure that they do not exonerate themselves too easily from the weight and gravity of their master's problematic act and especially that they will not think that praise for Alcestis for having *carried out her duty* (and we shall return to the antifeminist provocation that takes place here) will blur the injustice of their king's behavior. Indeed, the Handmaid does not finish before daring to hurl a blatantly sarcastic statement against her lord: "If he had died, he would have perished, but now that he has escaped he has such anguish as he will never forget."

Admetus's fan club chorus picks up the rebuke in the Handmaid's words and, constantly concerned about Admetus's public relations, is worried that the selfishness of his act should appear too brutal and revealing. It asks immediately: "Admetus is surely groaning at this trouble, at having to lose his noble wife?" The chorus tries to balance out Alcestis's sacrifice by stressing Admetus's pain and agony, and to play off the one against the other. But the Handmaid will have nothing of it. True, Admetus is weeping, but his tears are futile. In other words, he cannot cancel out the death of his wife, except by relinquishing the sacrifice she is making for him, which is one thing he is unwilling to do.

Up to this point, the moral map of the play has been drawn with a gentle and efficient hand. We have been given a vague preliminary promise of a happy ending so that our anger at Admetus does not reach a level that will prevent us from noticing new and original motives for his act. I stress *new* and *original* motives because the attempt—via the support chorus—at clouding the gravity of Admetus's act by lavishing words of praise on Alcestis and even by hinting obscenely at her "duty" is firmly neutralized by the Handmaid's most impressive appearance and heartrending descriptions, which bring the drama back to its origins: Alcestis is about to die, and her death is a blatant injustice. True, Admetus is pained and suffering, but can his pain provide moral atonement for his act? Still, through a special kind of intensity, his supporters persist on this path. They direct the audience, who are morally indecisive between censure and acceptance, to look toward Admetus's current suffering, and by using demagogic deceit, they wrap the husband with his wife's death robes, as if he, too, were about to die. They then call on the gods to save Admetus and rescue him from death, as if it were he, and not his wife, who were going to his death. With unequaled cynicism, they close the chapter thus: "Never shall I declare that marriage brings more happiness than sorrow. My evidence is past experience and the observation of the present misfortunes of the king, who is bereft of his excellent wife and will henceforth live a life unlivable."

This is scandalous talk. It is marriage, after all, that is saving Admetus from death, and there is nothing that can be said against it. Indeed, the king's tragedy—that is, the death of his wife—is also his salvation. And what is the meaning of the statement that his life will no longer be livable? Does mourning balance against death?

This is the new moral line of defense for Admetus's act, but does it have any chance at convincing us? At any minute, the heroes themselves will enter the stage, led by Admetus. He is pained and suffering, but in no way is he repentant.

In my opinion, it is here that Euripides takes a great risk with regard to Admetus's moral line of defense. He presents to us a hero who, although genuinely torn apart by the imminent death of his wife, is totally in denial as to the cause of her death and of his part in it, as if Alcestis's sacrifice were an element that cannot be questioned. Admetus talks to himself in terms of tragedy and death—the outcome of the approaching death of his wife. He speaks of his great love; he even urges his wife to pull herself together and not give in to death, as if it depended on her. He says that if she dies, he shall cease to exist (a more moderate version of what the chorus had to say about it when it compares real death with a "life that is unlivable").

He talks about sacred love. But Admetus does not mention his responsibility for his wife's death; he does not talk about the victim; he does not ask for her forgiveness; he does not offer to cancel the trade-off. In his words there is almost a total disregard for Alcestis's sacrifice, as if it were something to be taken for granted. This speech constitutes a stormy and dramatic junction in our moral map. It presents Admetus as being so convinced of the justice of his wife's sacrifice on his behalf and of his being worthy of it that he does not even bother to go back and check out either of these points. His wife's decision was a courageous and autonomous one, and he accepts and respects it: "Worthy is she of my honor, for she alone has died in my stead."

How simple and natural it would have been for the author of this drama to depict his hero at this moment, when the wife is about to carry out her sacrifice, as a man who is torn up and suffering in guilt over his actions, trying perhaps to repent, certainly to ask for forgiveness, maybe even threatening to kill himself in order to release his wife from her obligation to die. But Euripides did not choose this easy way out. What point is there to a hero who regrets, repents, and agonizes guiltily and uselessly at the very last moment? Such behavior and personality in his hero would have come across as lacking in seriousness and would have greatly reduced his value. Regret at such a late date would be interpreted as nothing other than manipulation. Euripides takes a different course, riskier from the point of view of trying to justify Admetus's behavior, but more profound from the point of view of presenting the couple's love relationship and their mutual ability to receive. Euripides takes a strong stance, impermeable even, with regard to Admetus's willingness to accept Alcestis's sacrifice to the extent that he does not even mention it at this stage. He allows Alcestis to give her *gift* completely, and by doing so he honors her image as a remarkable and wonderful wife. Thus, it is only natural that Admetus's love for his wife increases as her death

approaches, so much so that he actually begins—absurdly—
to blame Alcestis for giving herself up so easily to death; it is as if
the level of their love for each other is totally detached from the
trade-off.

During this mini-act, the reader experiences a conflicting emotional storm with regard to Admetus—on the one hand, annoyance
at the man's intransigence and his lack of apology for using words
such as "what a tragedy for both of us," but on the other hand, wonder at and even respect for his self-confidence regarding his acceptance of his wife's sacrifice. Admetus's moral code might be damaged,
but at least he is no hypocrite. Just when we are about to accept that
the moral swing between the two is such that the higher Alcestis
rises, the lower Admetus falls, Euripides puts us to a little test.

In her final, predeath monologue, Alcestis explains in detail the
significance of her sacrifice and the reasons why Admetus is more
important to her than she herself is. (Incidentally, Euripides does not
make things easier for himself in this cruel trade-off with death. He
does not hint that Alcestis owed anything to Admetus in return for
any special act of kindness he may have shown her or any member of
her family in the past. In this way, he maintains the purity and originality of Alcestis's sacrifice.) Indeed, Alcestis repeatedly stresses that
she is making her sacrifice of her own free will, notwithstanding the
fact that she considers it an injustice that Admetus's parents did not
see fit to die instead of him. Although she knows perfectly well that
there is no reparation equal to her sacrifice, she asks of her husband
just one thing—that he should not marry another after her death,
not because she is jealous of a new wife, but because she fears that a
stepmother would be harsh with her children.

Alcestis's reasoning with regard to a potential stepmother seems
rather far-fetched here and was certainly included for the purpose of
hiding in an indirect manner her natural and legitimate jealousy for
any woman who would inherit her position (as was already hinted).

But the fact that Alcestis is now making another condition in this trade-off (one, by the way, that is about to be disregarded in the near future, *but ironically it is its nonfulfillment that will bring about her salvation*) places a strange shadow on the perfection of her sacrifice. It seems that at the last moment, she is trying to hurt her husband, for whose sake she is sacrificing her life, and to punish and restrict him. True, as she has just said, Admetus is dearer to her than her own life, but she still plans to make sure that his suffering as a result of her death will be constant and continuous, so she is firm in her demand that he never marry another woman.

Interestingly enough—and here there is a fine psychological act on the part of the playwright—Admetus does not respond immediately to his dying wife's demand. Whether hesitant or confused by his wonderful wife, who at so painful a moment places conditions and justifies them with a far-fetched rationale, he falls into an embarrassed silence that immediately arouses his support chorus to respond in his stead. His supporters do not know exactly what should be done at this difficult juncture in order to reinstall in the king's damaged image a renewed lust for life. "Rest assured. I do not hesitate to speak on his behalf. He will do these things if he is in his right mind."

There is something ludicrous in the chorus's swift intervention, which makes commitments on Admetus's behalf before he even has a chance to open his mouth, an intervention that proves just how important this support chorus is in getting through this disgraceful trade-off affair with the minimum amount of conflict in order to swiftly remove it from the public agenda. Yet it is this "external" response on the part of the chorus that highlights the different response Admetus gives to his wife's request. He pays no attention to Alcestis's fears regarding a stepmother for her children because he clearly does not believe in those fears and is quite sure he can protect his children from any real or imagined ill-treatment on the part of a stepmother. Nor is he in any hurry to make promises that he has no intention to remarry in return for Alcestis's sacrifice. On the contrary, he emphasizes in his reply that so great is his love for his wife that she shall continue to be his wife even after death. He will not take a new wife, not as retribution to Alcestis, but as a natural and final response of one who remains faithful to his wife after her death: "there is no woman noble enough in birth or excellent enough in beauty. . . . This grief I will carry not for a year but as long as my life endures, dear wife."

He does not need conditions of gratefulness in order not to marry another woman. The love for his wife that fills his heart will not permit him to seek another woman, even after his wife's death. Throughout his monologue, Admetus differentiates between two elements of love and respect. His love is given to Alcestis because of what she is—her special beauty, her wisdom, and all her other outstanding qualities—whereas his respect is given her as a result of what she has done for him. But Alcestis still does not completely trust her husband even after the love-filled monologue and the oath of faithfulness, and uses her children as guarantees that their father will not remarry after she dies.

Strangely enough, the condition required by Alcestis is a logical and moral one, but it nevertheless somewhat clouds the glory of her sacrifice and perfection. Again, the condition comes across more as punishment for Admetus rather than a means to assure the health of her children, and we, who have already accepted her generosity as a fact, are entitled to wonder why this generosity cannot be complete and unconditional.

Admetus's personality is revealed here in all its complexity. He appears to be reticent, but he is also amazingly frank. Clearly he does not regret having entered the deal, nor is he playing a superficial game of regret. He is quite indifferent to public opinion. He accepts his wife's sacrifice as a matter of fact, wonderful indeed, but absolutely merited. There is no sign at this stage that he feels guilty about this sacrifice. He is a man who loves and is loved. Indeed, even if at this stage he were to renege on the cruel trade-off and say to his wife, "I'm not going through with it. Stay alive and I shall go to my death, as I should have in the first place," they would have been unable to return to the life they had at the beginning of the affair because it was no longer possible to blot out the exchange process. The second exchange, if the gods of Hades were at all agreeable, would not have simply canceled out the first exchange, but created a situation in which there were two exchanges, one on top of the other.

I believe that the fact that Admetus does not show any kind of doubt or regret, but takes the sacrifice as a given, actually eases things for Alcestis at this terrible time, when her soul is about to be carried off by death. If she chooses to sacrifice her life instead of her husband's, it would be better that her gift be complete and unhampered by the agonies of last-minute regrets. But is Admetus's unrelenting acceptance of this sacrifice at this stage no more than unbridled egoism, or does it also have confidence and moral persuasion? Does Admetus only take, or is he able also to give? We shall see this immediately in the third act.

Heracles arrives in town straight after Alcestis's death. Following a brief conversation with the chorus, to whom he tells of his difficult mission for the king of Thrace and of his great confidence in his physical powers and his ability to withstand the daring task that awaits him, he meets Admetus. When he notices the signs of mourning surrounding Admetus, Heracles tries to find out about the object of the king's mourning. The latter hedges and does not disclose that it is Alcestis who has died, although Heracles is aware of the forthcoming intervention on Alcestis's behalf. Admetus tries to play down the importance of the deceased and the mourning, claiming that it was only some woman who had died—in the hope that Heracles will not be put off visiting his home because it is in mourning. And indeed, Heracles is persuaded to enter Admetus's home.

Admetus is acting in a decidedly strange and seemingly unjustifiable manner. What is the point of welcoming Heracles into his home on this grim and horrible day of mourning, the day on which his beloved wife gave up her life on his behalf? Not only the warm welcome but also the way in which Admetus beats around the bush, refusing to supply Heracles with the real reason for the mourning and lying about the identity of the deceased, result in serious antipathy toward Admetus. Even the king's supporters, who until now had been trying to protect him, can no longer contain themselves and castigate him sharply: "What are you about? With such a calamity before you, Admetus, have you the heart to entertain guests? Why are you so foolish?"

Admetus understands the chorus's sharp rebuke, but excuses his behavior by saying that he does not wish to deny so generous a guest his hospitality. He is also thus obliged to lie about who has died so that Heracles will agree to stay at his palace. Admetus explains that his tragedy would be no smaller were Heracles to refuse hospitality at his home, whereas he, Admetus, would be seen as ungracious. Moreover, he feels a special obligation toward Heracles, who always makes him welcome at Argos.

This small act is of greatest importance not only because Heracles will subsequently save Alcestis from the jaws of death and return her safely into her husband's arms in return for this generous welcome, but because it helps us to better understand Admetus's unique personality and the way in which he rationalizes his actions. Admetus is absolutely autonomous and independent in his moral judgments: "Would this new evil be added to the others, that my house should be called guest-hating."

Admetus is well aware that the public is scrutinizing him in minute detail. He knows that it is in his interest to carry out meticulously the mourning ritual for Alcestis and not merely to suffer his own grim agonies, but also to show them publicly. Otherwise, he might be seen as ungrateful or—heaven forbid—unloving toward the woman who has sacrificed her life for him. But Admetus does not depend on public opinion and its external trappings. To him, the demands of hospitality are more important than his personal image. He feels profoundly the power of his mourning, and he is sure of his great love for Alcestis, as he was sure of his wife's love for him. Admetus is depicted as a man who is genuine and generous, although at this moment this generosity places his personal image in jeopardy. A man who is fully aware of the difference between good and bad, he is doing what he thinks has to be done, until the chorus, which has only just finished berating him for what he has done, is convinced of the justice of his deeds and closes with: "In nobility is all wisdom. I wonder, but in my soul abides the trust that the god-fearing man shall do well."

The fourth act, which deals with the sharp conflict between Admetus and his father over the entire trade-off affair, is about to begin. It is a fierce and complex conflict. The father, Pheres, voices his complaints not only in theory, but as one who refutes unequivocally the accusations his son hurls at him. Our hero enters this conflict in a lucid manner befitting his personality and the way in which he makes his decisions. We sense that he is secure within his own moral code. We might not be particularly keen on this moral code, which might even be the result of emotional impregnability, but it is clearly a personal code that Admetus does not attempt to adapt in accordance with public opinion.

If Euripides' final objective in this drama was to engender a consensus in support of Admetus's morbid trade-off with his wife Alcestis and to prove that the boundaries of a relationship between a man and a woman are extremely broad, then this is no simple objective. Indeed, the playwright acted wisely when he chose to wait until the drama is well into its second half to voice his sharpest criticism against Admetus's act. Had the criticism been voiced at an earlier stage, it would have so blotted out Admetus's act that it would have been absolutely impossible to rehabilitate the moral trust that we are demanded to give him. The fierce conflict that evolves between Pheres and Admetus takes place at a time when we have a complex and nonunilateral feeling toward Admetus's personality. We are still far from condoning his act, but we can sense the confidence of a man who knows how to *receive* because he knows also how to *give*. For him, receiving is a kind of giving. His ability to accept his wife's sacrifice evolves not only because he loves himself (and self-love is certainly a sound basis for a healthy psyche), but because he respects the other's gift and has faith in the giver and her generosity. We shall see this attitude at the end of the drama, when Admetus puts his faith in Heracles and agrees to take the strange, veiled woman from him despite his emotional reticence and notwithstanding the enormous damage that this acquiescence can cause him, again, in the opinion of a public that is examining him so closely.

At the beginning of the fourth act, Pheres, Admetus's father, arrives for Alcestis's funeral. It is a complicated and embarrassing moment for him, and he requires great powers of diplomacy in order to get through it. (Admetus's mother is probably afraid to show herself and to cope with the situation.) On the one hand, the father is still angry with his son for having forced him to face such a challenge to die in his place—which he firmly rejected—but on the other hand, he is gratified that Alcestis agreed to the sacrifice, thus saving him the hardship and confusion and sorrow involved in the death of his son, whose life he refused to save by agreeing to die in his place. In spite of his tense and difficult relationship with his son, he feels duty bound to be present at this troubled time, when his son leads his wife to her funeral.

Pheres does not discuss his relationship with his son, but tries to join the general consensus. In other words, he heaps praise on Alcestis, to whom, in order to sweeten her journey to Hades, he brings some new adornments that will protect her in her grave. But behind his words of praise, some other and far less pleasant expressions begin to escape from his mouth, the worst of which come at the end of his speech: "Such marriages are profitable to mankind, I declare, or to marry is not worthwhile." This is a revolting thing to say, and it reflects more than a little misogyny. Strangely enough, however, he does not, at this stage, morally reject the idea that one person should sacrifice herself on behalf of another.

Admetus, deeply depressed and guilt stricken, hurls a coarse outburst against his father, who could have spared him this terrible hour by sacrificing himself instead. He lists all the reasons why it would have been more suitable for one of his parents to have died in his stead and insists that the fact that Alcestis agreed to the sacrifice is proof that this kind of deal is possible and even honors the dead.

Admetus continues in full swing and causes his father to lose his equilibrium. So furious is Admetus that he announces to his parents—how timely, just as he is burying his beloved wife—that he does not intend to support them in their old age, nor will he arrange their funerals. Altogether, he tells his father, they can cease seeing him as their son. As far as he is concerned, he has carried out all his obligations toward them. After all, if they were prepared to let him die, then to them he is as good as dead. They will not be allowed to benefit from the sacrifice of a beautiful young woman, while they, old and soon to die, refused to undertake the same sacrifice.

The chorus is greatly disconcerted by Admetus's words and tries to soften them, but it is too late. Now, when the matter itself is being laid bare to moral discussion, there is no choice but to leave nothing unsaid. Pheres is aflame with anger and justifies himself furiously against his son's accusations. "Don't you die for my sake, and I shan't die for yours. You are glad to see the light. Do you suppose your father isn't?" the father cries out in fury and then adds, "You fought shamelessly to save your life, and you are alive because you eluded the lot that was fated for you and killed this woman. Then do you speak of my cowardice, you vilest of cowards, who are worsted by a woman, who died for the sake of a fine young fellow like you?"

But when Admetus continues to stand his ground—"Is it the same thing for a man in his prime to die as for an old man?"—Pheres asks observantly, "And aren't you burying this corpse [who is younger than you] instead of yourself?" Admetus's response—"Proof of your cowardice, vile creature"—is of course dubious and far-fetched.

Here, seemingly, Admetus's defeat could be complete, and Pheres need utter not another word. But the moral swing between Admetus and Alcestis does not work on a single axis; in other words, the higher Alcestis rises in adulation, the lower Admetus falls in condemnation, but on a second axis he also interestingly stays parallel with her. Alcestis's virtues reflect on Admetus as someone who was at least worthy of her sacrifice.

There is no doubt that Pheres is very disturbed morally at Alcestis's having agreed to sacrifice herself. Although at first he heaped warm rhetoric on Alcestis's virtues, once he is told that her sacrifice was the result of his cowardice, he tries to prove that her personal sacrifice had nothing to do with nobility, but was based on two decidedly inferior elements: Admetus's cunning in persuading his wife to die in his stead and the woman's stupidity for agreeing to it. ("*She was not shameless; her you found foolish.*")

Naturally, these attacks on Alcestis, whose body is lying in state before the crowd, cancel out all possibility of further dialogue. An appalled Admetus curses his parents and banishes his father, and the chorus, after vain attempts at pacifying the two hawks, bursts into songs of praise for Alcestis as if by doing so they can protect the dead woman and purify her against Pheres' scorn.

Euripides touches on a very important issue regarding the moral norms within a family framework and especially those within a marital framework. Of all life's many spheres, I believe family and marriage relationships are the richest for resolving moral dilemmas. Here, and to a lesser degree in working relationships, man's morals are put to the test. Because ties of mutual love and dependency are so characteristic of family relationships, moral balances become fine, complex, and painful. It is easy in family life and in marital relationships for immoral situations to develop involving extortion, control, and sacrifice that are not based on equality. On the other hand, however, neither is the question of equality in marriage technical or formal because the power of love lies in its attempts to prove itself in a way that is impossible to measure and to examine according to criteria of equal rights and obligations.

In order to create strong emotional involvement in moral and psychological dilemmas, literature frequently tries to exaggerate the human situations in which the fictitious characters are placed. But as readers, we must not let these extreme situations confuse us; we must rather try to pick out from them meanings applicable to less-extreme situations and to issues that contain within them similar conflicting patterns. Altogether, let's examine ourselves: Are we prepared to accept as moral the sacrifice of a mother who gives her life—at a time of war, say—in order to save that of her child and to approve the morality of a child who accepts its mother's sacrifice, but refuse to give similar moral approval to a woman who does the same thing for her husband merely because he seems to us to be stronger and we fear that he has taken advantage of her weakness?

Alcestis sacrifices her life for her husband, and her husband is willing to accept her sacrifice. If this acceptance is immoral, then perhaps the giving is also immoral; quite possibly, a person does not have the right to sacrifice her life for another. If this is so, then not only is Pheres right in calling Alcestis "foolish," but he should also go so far as to denounce her morally. Euripides places in Pheres' mouth the sharpest possible condemnation of Admetus, but because Pheres also gets carried away in his angry condemnation of Alcestis, the condemnation boomerangs against his just claims. In defending Alcestis from Pheres' condemnation, the chorus is also—in a round-about way—defending Admetus.

While Admetus sets out on Alcestis's funeral procession, Heracles discovers in a conversation with a manservant that Admetus has hidden the fact of Alcestis's death in order not to deter Heracles from visiting his home. It is important to stress here that Admetus does not withhold information on Alcestis's death out of remorse at the trade-off deal between him and his wife. This trade-off was already known to Heracles even before his arrival at Admetus's palace. Heracles is very agitated at the fact that in order to meet the demands of hospitality, Admetus has tried to hide from him the news of his wife's death, and he sees this act not only as extremely noble of Admetus, but also as especially courageous in the face of public opinion that condemns him and lies in wait for every act that so much as hints at disrespect for the deceased. As a symbol of his thanks, Heracles decides to set out immediately to rescue Alcestis from Hades and to bring her back to Earth, alive and well.

In the meantime, Admetus returns from Alcestis's funeral, and the agony of his mourning bursts out in all its force. Now that he is left without Alcestis to defend their trade-off with death, he finds himself more exposed and vulnerable to his public's condemnation. It is as if only at this moment does he understand the seriousness of his act. The chorus tries to comfort him: "Your life was happy, you did not know what sorrow was, and then came this blow. But you have saved your life. Your wife has died, has left her life behind. Is this so strange? Many men has death separated from their wives."

This is the first time that his supporters allude clearly to the trade-off; until now they have tried to blur the matter, which just goes to show how considered their words were not in accordance with devotion to the truth, but in accordance with the clear interest of defending the king's image. Indeed, when they see that Admetus is sinking deeper and deeper into his sorrow, now, after the funeral, at a time when public opinion would have preferred him to maintain a low profile, they are trying to remind him that his life was saved by the same death over which he is grieving so profoundly.

Admetus is not thinking about public opinion, but about the terrible void in which he now finds himself after his wife's decease, which proves once again that such trade-offs can be understood and defended only within the mutual and intimate moral code of a husband and wife. When one of them dies, the other will remain vulnerable to a kind of censure that is virtually impossible to bear: "I regard my wife's fate as happier than my own, though it might not seem to be so. Her no pain will ever touch again; she has surcease of many toils, and with glory. I, on the other hand, who ought not to have lived, have escaped destiny, but shall drag out a bitter life. Too late to realize it."

The question is, Why did Admetus not understand all this earlier, when he agreed to his wife's sacrifice? Could it have been that then, before her death, he only pretended not to understand, fearing that full realization of what he was about to do would have prevented him from doing it? "That any man who happens to be unfriendly to me will say: 'Look at the fellow who keeps alive so shamefully; he had not the encourage to die, but gave in exchange the woman he married, in his cowardice and escaped Hades. Do you call that a man? He hates his parents, though he himself was not willing to die.'"

This is a very significant moment in our drama. We must decide if the pain and sorrow in Admetus's confessions are a superficial, staged performance or whether they are frank and genuine. It is quite obvious to us that Admetus has no interest in attacking himself thus in public; on the contrary, he would prefer to smooth over and forget the entire incident. We understand that this powerful guilt he is now feeling is indeed sincere and is the result of his *sense of loss* for Alcestis, in whose giving and sacrifice he placed all his faith, and who in life would have been able to present a moral defense of the trade-off.

Yes, the faith Admetus has in his wife and in his friends is the motif with which the play comes to an end. We all hold our breaths the moment Heracles arrives with Alcestis wrapped in a shawl and asks Admetus to take her to his home. We understand how difficult it is for Admetus to comply with Heracles' request and bring this woman into his palace, not only because of his profound grief over the recent loss of his wife, but because of his promise to Alcestis that after her death he would never touch another woman. Yet, we know that all Admetus has to do is take this veiled woman into his home, and he will be bringing Alcestis back from the dead. We simply do not understand, but sense with all the power of our fear, how good it is that Admetus is a man who does not consider public opinion and what people will say, but acts according to his own instincts; how good that the man before us is willing to renege on a promise he made to his wife, who was so beloved and precious to him, because he has so much faith in the request-gift of a true friend.

The final scene is a truly wonderful work of art. With the power of identity, Euripides turns us into accomplices in Admetus's breach of trust, and in doing so, he is paving our way, in the most correct and accurate way, to understanding (and, who knows, maybe even to accepting) the moral codes that guide Admetus. Thus, the announcement at the close of the play—*"I am fortunate"*—does not in the end revolt us. I must, though, be accurate and reserved here: it does not revolt *me* in the end. As I have already said, in moral commentary and in literature as in real life, the final decision as to respect or censure must remain with each and every reader in accordance with his or her own scale of moral values.

❧ 3 ☙

The Absurd as a Moral Guide

"THE GUEST,"
BY ALBERT CAMUS

"The Guest," from Albert Camus's *Exile and the Kingdom*, takes place in Algiers—while it is still under French domination—during the early 1950s. We can already sense the first signs of the local Arab revolt against French colonialism, and there is new tension in the air. Unlike other French overseas colonies, Algiers was home to a very large expatriate French community. This community started settling there at the beginning of the nineteenth century and considered it to be their homeland, in every sense of the word. One such Frenchman is a schoolteacher called Daru, sent to a small school on a barren hilltop in one of the country's more remote provinces on the edge of the Sahara desert. This local school also serves as a home to Daru, who is unmarried, and its single classroom is attended by children from all the villages in the region.

Our story begins one afternoon when a county policeman called Balducci arrives at the school with an Arab prisoner who murdered his cousin. It is autumn, and a heavy snowfall has caused havoc with the roads; for three days, no children have come to school. Having brought the Arab from one of the neighboring villages but obliged to return forthwith to his own village, where things are getting out of control, Balducci asks Daru to take the Arab to the nearest large town. Daru refuses to undertake the mission, but Balducci decides to

41

leave the prisoner with Daru, anyway, probably in the belief that Daru will have a change of heart eventually and take him to the authorities who are waiting for him in the county capital.

Daru, however, has no intention of changing his mind. He feeds the Arab and lets him sleep in his room, but hopes that he will escape and thus release him (Daru) from a task he has no intention of carrying out. But the prisoner does not escape, and the following morning Daru leads him to the edge of the desert, supplies him with food and money, and points him in the direction of the desert nomads, who will give him shelter. But the prisoner chooses not to escape. Alone, he climbs up the hill leading to the county capital, where he is awaited by representatives of the law.

Daru returns to the silent schoolhouse, where he finds a message on the blackboard, written in chalk by an uneducated hand, presumably one of the Arab's relatives: "You handed over our brother. You will pay for this." A deep sense of loneliness engulfs him, and the story ends with the words, "In this vast landscape he had loved so much, he was alone."

Let us look at the end of the story and ask ourselves, What do we feel from a moral point of view about the behavior of this schoolmaster? Does his stubborn decision not to hand over the Arab to the authorities and to allow him to escape into the desert seem to us to be a moral decision or not, a positive or a negative decision? If it seems to us positive, how shall we rationalize its motives? Do we empathize with what the schoolmaster did? And what is the extent of this empathy? Supposing we do not empathize with Daru's behavior, do we get the feeling from reading the story carefully that Daru himself considered his decision not to hand over the Arab to the authorities to be a positive, moral one? If this was indeed his feeling, what were the reasons that motivated him?

We shall put these questions to the test in our review of this story, which, like most of Camus's stories—such as his long novella *The*

Stranger and the novel *The Plague*—is written in a style that is terse, accurate, and dry, with a minimum of psychological reasoning. It is the kind of writing that is known as existentialist and, I would say, even barren—writing that tries to drive through sharp, although not necessarily extreme, human situations to the very backbone of human existence.

To the first question—Does the reader manage to form a positive moral empathy with Daru's behavior?—I can offer only a personal reply. I can testify that after a first reading of this story and possibly also a second one, I felt a clear sense of empathy as a reader for the way Daru behaved toward the Arab. It seemed to me to be the right thing to do, even though I did not ignore the problematic aspects. The fact that the Arab prisoner decides to cross the desert alone in order to hand himself in to the authorities seemed to me to be a situation of supreme morality. Moreover, I can say from personal experience that many of the students who studied this story with me felt a similar intuitive reaction.[1]

But, again, although the reader's moral reaction is determined within his or her own personal sphere and in accordance with his or her own moral criteria, there is a clear indication that the text of "The Guest" is much in support of the view that Daru is morally activated. Whether his motivation is correct or just is another question; from Daru's point of view, however, even if he is motivated by ignorance, the framework within which his activity takes place seems to prove that he is not acting out of any personal motives, but out of a sense of morality.

A close review of this story has shown me that Daru himself has *no* explanation for his behavior. Furthermore, by using a dry but accurate form of artistic minimalism, the author actually neutralizes any

---

1. We must remember that the first encounter with a work of literature is crucial. Moreover, in many cases, the first encounter is also the only one.

possible motivation for Daru's behavior, so the natural conclusion is that there is no reason for his decision to free the murderer. In other words, it is an absurd decision, if we can define absurd as something that has no purpose. Nonetheless—and here we are faced with the uniqueness of the story—this clearly absurd act is conceived not only by Daru but also by many of us as an act that is moral. Why?

The teacher watches the two men climbing up the hill toward him. From here on, he is referred to either by name or as "the teacher." The fact that he is referred to as "the teacher" hints to us that here is a man who teaches rules; moreover, as an elementary school teacher, he is probably also expected in his day-to-day dealings with his pupils to supply answers to questions regarding behavioral norms and moral principles. This is a man who by his speech and actions proves that he has considerable inner autonomy, a conclusion perhaps also supported by the autonomy and loneliness required of a teacher in a remote school such as the one in this story and by the intellectual stance that he develops toward his environment.

Had our hero been a farmer or a local tradesman, we may have said that his decision not to hand over the prisoner is based on an ingrained principle of hospitality that cannot be transgressed or on the selfish interests of one who does not want any trouble with his neighbors. But this is the not the case with the teacher, whose salary is paid by the authorities and who is thus not dependent on the local community for his livelihood. On the contrary, the schoolyard is full of haystacks, sent by the French government for him to distribute among the needy, drought-stricken country folks. The locals are dependent on him, not he on them. His decision can thus be perfectly free, and indeed it is.

The situation in "The Guest" brings to mind a story with a similar structure, "Matthew Falcon" by Prosper Mérimée. The story involves a criminal who escapes to a country estate, where he comes across the beloved son of the absent owner of the estate, a nobleman highly respected in his community. The criminal asks the boy to hide him from the law, and the boy complies. When the police arrive, headed by an officer who is the boy's uncle, they sense that the criminal has been hidden by the boy, and they coax him, with the help of a glittering gold watch, into giving away the criminal's hiding place. When the father, the noble estate owner, returns and hears about the affair, not only does he destroy the gold watch, but he also executes his son for breaching the code of hospitality by which he was bound. This story is founded on clear-cut fundamental codes of hospitality, and I have mentioned it in order to point out the profound differences between the two stories. Daru has no fundamental code of hospitality or of nonbetrayal. Nor did the Arab escape to Daru's home in order to ask for shelter; he was brought there by a French policeman.

Who, therefore, is this Daru? Does his decision not to extradite the Arab murderer to the authorities stem from the romantic outlook of a man who secludes himself from society, an eccentric whose anarchistic opinions reject conventions of law and order? If we take a careful look at the information supplied in the story about Daru, we shall see that he is far from being such a person. Daru is a schoolteacher, sent to work in this remote region on the edge of the desert. He arrived after World War II, asking for a post in the little town at the base of the foothills separating the plateaus from the desert, but because no such post was available, he was sent farther north, on the plateau itself, where the silence and the solitude were at first extremely difficult for him to bear. He did not choose this extreme solitude out of a desire to cut himself off from society or as one who seeks seclusion for the sake of it. It is possible, however, that his constant contact with the barren and exposed wastelands affects his "absurd decision." The decision is an instinctive reaction, an existentialist reaction, in all its prosaic but suggestive meaning, which says that existence precedes awareness.

Again, the period is that of the early days of the Algerian revolt against French colonialism, and the prisoner in question is an Arab, handed over by a French policeman (albeit a Corsican and himself a member of a minority) to a Frenchman. Can it be that the national struggle is the reason behind Daru's decision not to deliver the Arab to police headquarters? Is he a Frenchman who secretly supports the Algerian struggle and whose sympathy for the Arab is his way of protesting against the injustice of French rule in Algiers? When this story was published in the 1950s, the political rationale seemed to be the most logical explanation for Daru's behavior, but the information supplied in the story contradicts any hypothesis that political dissent connected with the colonial conflict is the drive behind that strange behavior. Daru himself is no pacifist, nor is he a man who is alien to the French society to which he belongs. In his small apartment, he keeps a gun, and he will certainly be prepared to fight, yes, but only if necessary. Earlier, when the elderly gendarme tries to persuade him to undertake the mission and says, "In wartime people do all kinds of jobs," Daru replies with a tinge of irony: "Then I'll wait for the decla- ration of war!" In other words, Daru does not deny solidarity with his nation, France. When the time comes, he will fight alongside every- one else. Indeed, he asks Balducci the kind of question a French citi- zen would ask: "Is he against us?" And the policeman's reply, "I don't think so, but you can never be sure," is totally noncommittal.

The assumption that hidden support for the Algerian uprising is what motivates Daru's intransigent decision to release the Arab pris- oner has no foundation in the text itself. Daru reveals no signs of any special sympathy for the local Arabs; he looks upon them in a clearly sober and realistic way. For him, France is not only the metropolis that pays his salary, it is also obviously his cultural context. A small detail shows us this connection. At the beginning of the story, there is a description of the classroom in which he teaches; here, says the author, the blackboard still sports a map of France, her four major rivers marked in four different-colored chalks. There is no greater contrast than between the geography of France, with her rivers and fertile soil, and the aridness of the desert surrounding Daru's habitat. But this distinction is the material that Daru teaches the young Algerians, who surely also memorize it by heart—like the inhabitants of other French colonies: we are the descendants of the early Gauls. Daru comes across as an obedient and conventional teacher, who has no special sympathy in his heart for the Arabs that would cause him to behave as he does.

We shall return later to the author's sophistication in choosing an Arab prisoner, a choice that allows him to drug our contention and to slide the absurd into a sense of moral sympathy. If the murderer were a Frenchman rather than an Arab, it might have been difficult for us to forgive Daru for his refusal to hand over the prisoner to the authorities. But I believe that once our analysis of the story is completed, we shall be forced to admit, based on the inner spirit of the text, that had the elderly policeman brought a French murderer rather than an Arab one, Daru would have acted in exactly the same way. His decision has nothing to do with the conflict between the two communities in Algiers, even though this conflict does float vaguely above the story and could confuse the reader's understanding of Daru's true motives.

Perhaps the reason behind the nonbetrayal stems not from the prisoner's nationality but from the crime he committed or perhaps from his character or his personality. Who is this Arab, and what is his crime?

He is a murderer who killed his cousin because of a family squabble over grain. "He killed his cousin with a billhook. You know, like a sheep, *kreezk!*" There was no ideology involved in this murder, nor did it occur because of some inner code of tribal revenge or family honor, a concept that is apparently—and as far as I am concerned, only apparently—inaccessible to Western mentality. It is a primary crime, an act that is absolutely evil according to any moral criteria: murder of a blood relative for the sake of financial gain. It seems to me that readers who try to define Daru's decision not to hand over the prisoner as a nonjudgmental stance toward people or acts belonging to another culture—often a so-called inferior culture— will not find what they want in this story. First of all, Daru is no stranger to Arab culture; he is hardly a European liberal full of Western guilt who believes that the murder of one Arab by another is an act of little significance and not worthy of attention. On the contrary, upon being told by the policeman about the murder, "Daru felt a sudden wrath against the man, against all men with their rotten spite, their tireless hates, their blood lust."

Daru is not lacking in judgment and knows how to differentiate between good and bad. His moral reaction is powerful and immediate. Nonetheless, he does not want to hand this Arab over to the authorities, and the main question is, once again, Why?

Many stories have been written about people with powerful social consciences who find themselves in situations in which they are forced to cooperate with criminals, to harbor them in their homes and avoid handing them over to the law. But such stories are usually built on an interactive relationship that develops between the innocent, law-abiding bystander and a criminal who has managed suddenly to penetrate his world—a relationship based on the "charm" the lawbreaker has on the "square" citizen or on the criminal's "seeing the light" and experiencing an inner revolution after intimate and humane contact with the decent world. But such a relationship is foreign to our story. Daru's decision precedes his personal familiarity with the Arab. As soon as Balducci issues his request and before Daru has had any kind of conversation with the prisoner, he has already stated categorically that he has no intention of taking the man to the police headquarters at Tinguit. And during the night that the two spend together in the schoolhouse, he shows no signs of friendship toward the Arab, who does try to form a bond with the teacher. As a person, the Arab does not arouse in him any interest. He asks Daru to accompany him to the prison, but Daru refuses. Even at the dramatic moment when he stops the Arab and points out the two paths he can take, the one to freedom in the desert and the other to the town where the courthouse awaits him and ultimately jail, the Arab turns toward him in a sort of panic and says, "Listen," and Daru replies dryly, "No, be quiet. Now I'm leaving you."

In other words, no real personal or spiritual bond develops in the course of the story between Daru and the prisoner in his custody that can justify in retrospect the decision not to give him up. Moreover, the Arab does not appear to repent his crime so that it is impossible to adopt a rather doubtful interpretation that Daru does not hand him in because he considers the prisoner's inner repentance to be of more value than incarceration in jail.

> "Why did you kill him?" he asked in a voice whose hostile tone surprised him.
>
> The Arab looked away.
>
> "He ran away. I ran after him."
>
> He raised his eyes to Daru gain and they were full of a sort of woeful interrogation. "Now what will you do to me?"
>
> "Are you afraid?"
>
> He stiffened, turning his eyes away.
>
> "Are you sorry?"
>
> The Arab stared at him openmouthed. Obviously he did not understand.

The personality of the Arab murderer does not give us even a hint of a reason for not handing him over. Camus goes to great lengths not to arouse in us any kind of sympathy for the Arab.

Perhaps we should go off on another track altogether—not to

seek out the reason for the nonextradition in Daru's or the Arab's personalities, but to a point of view that rejects, in principle, anything
to do with the law. In other words, Daru's behavior is similar to that
of another of Camus's heroes, Taru, in the novel *The Plague*, who is
also outspokenly opposed to the death sentence for any reason. Daru
is an anarchist who rejects the law. If the case were similar in "The
Guest," the law should have been presented here as brutal and
threatening, but it is not. Rarely is a representative of the law
depicted in so pleasant and humanitarian a form as is the elderly
gendarme.

Balducci is a gentle and humane man. He is himself a member of
an ethnic minority in France and is quite devoid of the arrogance
characteristic of the ruling majority. When he leads the prisoner
across the desert, he does it on horseback, with his prisoner following on foot, tied to him. But the Corsican takes the trouble to pace
the horse so as not to wear out the Arab. When they arrive at the
schoolhouse, and Daru offers to release the prisoner from his bonds,
Balducci is quick to agree, and his words sound so human, coming
from the mouth of a policeman: "I don't like it either. You don't get
used to putting a rope on a man even after years of it, and you're even
ashamed—yes, ashamed. But you can't let them have their way."

An old policeman, who has never become used to tying up a man,
and is still ashamed when he has to do so, is a policeman who represents the most human side of the law. Indeed, Daru, whom he treats
as he would his own son, appears to be very fond of him. Balducci
presents the law in the most honest and fair way—"you can't let
them have their way." Nor does he ask Daru to lock up the prisoner
or to judge him. All he asks is for Daru to deliver him to the police
authorities who are waiting to try him in the nearest county town.

A well-known story in Hebrew literature written some years before Camus's story is similar in several ways. I refer to S. Yizhar's "The
Prisoner," in which the hero has to decide whether to release an Arab

shepherd or to take him to a prisoners' compound a long way away, after having been shocked at the hedonistic brutality that accompanied the prisoner's interrogation at the hands of the hero's fellow soldiers. But in that story, it is clear that the soldier's moral dilemma has to do with the unexpected behavior of his colleagues, whereas in Camus's story, the teacher is resolute in his decision, notwithstanding the fact that his heart shrinks with sympathy for his friend the gendarme, who is deeply offended by his refusal.

Are we faced here with a little man trying to avoid sudden and unfamiliar responsibility, a man who says, "It's none of my business. Leave me alone"? In fact, several sentences in the story would support such a view of Daru, but if this is so, what do we find moral about people who refuse to help others in trouble, to take care of a wounded comrade, or to hold onto an escaped criminal until the arrival of the police? Can we muster respect for such people, or, alternatively, do we scorn them?

The situation here is also not one in which an urban policeman asks a passer-by to watch over a suspect until he is able to call for back-up forces, and the passer-by, in a hurry to get away, refuses "to do the policeman's job." Daru refuses not because he is in a hurry to involve himself in something else or is disturbed in the middle of a task. His refusal is an ideological refusal. Moreover, Daru does not merely take a passive stance of not handing over the prisoner, but a blatantly active stand that makes it possible for the Arab to choose the option of escaping into the desert. He equips the prisoner with food and money so that he can make his way to the desert nomads, who will give him safe shelter.

If all our unsuccessful efforts at finding a reason for Daru's behavior have been refuted by the story's precise and lucid text, then perhaps there is some profound and wonderful hidden reason connected to the fact that Daru is passively using his talents as an educator to get the Arab *to hand himself in*, as indeed happens at the end of the story. In other words, Daru creates a situation in which the Arab is given two options, to escape or to be punished, in the belief that if the man really feels his guilt, he will give himself up to the authorities, which is the highest possible moral level.

Let us recall the wonderful ending of Dostoyevsky's *Crime and Punishment*, when Raskolnikov takes himself to the police station to admit his crime in spite of the fact that no one—including the investigator who identified the crime—has any clear-cut and unequivocal proof against him. In "The Guest," too, we are witnessing at the end of the story a brilliant picture of morality, in which the murderer walks alone in the desert toward the police who are awaiting him, although escape was within his reach.

However, we are unfortunately obliged to reject this beautiful option as well, which would have given Daru pedagogic power and explained his action. After leaving the Arab at the crossroads, he discovers on his return to the schoolhouse that the Arab did not choose to escape into the desert, but to make his own way to the police authorities waiting for him in Tinguit. The words of the author—"And in that slight haze, Daru, with heavy heart, made out the Arab walking slowly on the road to prison"[2]—indicate, however, that this *self*-imprisonment on the part of the Arab is not the hidden outcome Daru was hoping for.

In conclusion, slowly but surely we are discovering that Camus's simple but dry text is ruling out, gently but accurately, all possible explanations that we can conceive of for Daru's steadfast early decision not to hand the Arab over to the police authorities. Because there is no reason available, we are able to say that his act is unmotivated or absurd. The decision is not understood by the gendarme, not understood by the Arab, not understood even by Daru himself. The only sentence that attempts to explain Daru's behavior says, "That man's

2. In the French original, it is "Le coeur serré," which means "painful heart."

stupid crime revolted him, but to hand him over was contrary to honour. Merely thinking of it made him smart with humiliation."

But this explanation is extremely obtuse and totally meaningless. What does the author mean by honor? Whose honor? Honor for the murderer? What for? What kind of honor would be affronted if the prisoner is led to the courtroom, where he will be rightly and truthfully judged?

An act of the absurd or an act that cannot be justified at all is an act that cannot serve as a moral example because it cannot be translated into another set of conventions that says, "If such and such is the case, then what should happen is so and so." Despite the lack of justification, despite the fact that all the elements in this story do not justify his act, we nonetheless accept the schoolteacher's absurd act as a moral one.

Daru is unfamiliar with Camus's philosophy, which says, "I am shouting that I believe in nothing and that everything is absurd, except that I cannot doubt my shouting, and I may just as well believe at least in my protest. Revolt is the first and only proof that I am given in this way in the very midst of the absurd experience." Daru is not an intellectual, acting out a theoretical philosophy. He is a simple schoolteacher, in whom the sense of the world's absurdity is instilled through his isolated meeting with a barren landscape, which is described with great power on several occasions in the story:

This is what the region was like, cruel to live in, even without men—who didn't make matters any better, either. But Daru had been born here. Everywhere else, he felt exiled.

This is the way it was: bare rock covered three quarters of the region. Towns sprang up, flourished, then disappeared; men came by, loved one another or fought bitterly then died. No-one in this desert, neither he nor his guest, mattered. And yet, outside this desert neither of them, Daru knew, could have really lived.

The absurdity of the universe is part of Daru's emotional experience, so that his reaction, too, is absurd because only an absurd reaction is worthy of an absurd universe. Perhaps it is the sense of honor that he feared would be harmed or desecrated through some incorrect act—the honor of someone who moves between an absurd and meaningless world and an act that is meaningless. Marceaux, the hero of the novella *The Stranger*, acts in a similarly absurd manner, killing the Arab for no reason or, as he explains later at his trial, because of the sun. The same absurd reaction that results in a totally unnecessary death in *The Stranger*, however, rolls matters toward an act that has moral validity in "The Guest." It leads the murderer alone in the desert toward the prison that awaits him.

There is no chance of understanding Daru's behavior. His absurd decision creates misunderstanding all around him, not only in the Arab or in the old gendarme or even in Daru himself, but also among the Arab's relatives, who come to the empty schoolhouse and leave a message on the board saying, "You handed over our brother. You will pay for this." An absurd stance cannot but reflect a feeling of isolation, and so, indeed, it is with a deep sense of loneliness that the story comes to an end.

Had the story ended with the Arab escaping into the desert, we would almost certainly have felt no moral sympathy for Daru's behavior. It is the fact that in the end the Arab gives himself up that ensures Daru's absurd decision our attention and our trust. But when we try to examine whether there was ever a clear-cut connection between the teacher's intentions and behavior and the story's final outcome—a murderer walks alone in the desert and gives himself up—not only do we see no such connection, but on the contrary we discover that the moral act that takes place at the end of the story actually contradicts the hero's intentions.

The story's rhetorical system, as it is revealed throughout, makes sure on the one hand to instill in us a kind of illusion that Daru has real reasons for not handing in the Arab, while on the other hand systematically and determinedly uprooting any possibility of presenting concrete reasoning of any kind for Daru's decision. Camus accomplishes this illusion mainly by choosing an Arab to play the role of murderer in order to take advantage of our sympathy for the Algerian uprising—the "liberal racism" that has it that an Arab is not punishable by anyone from the West—in order to dull any opposition to Daru's absurdity. In describing a situation of isolation, the illusion is created in the story that Daru is some kind of social rebel, a romantic hermit, trying to shake himself free of the demands of society, thus making it possible to identify with his behavior. But all these deceptions are merely temporary, and the text constantly makes sure to dispel each of them with speed and accuracy so that Daru's decision—which is an absurd, existential, irrational, grave, and uncompromising decision—can overcome the reader's rational obstructions and form in his heart sympathy and support not only for Daru's experience but for his position also.

In realistic situations in which we judge morality according to objectives, means, and overall reasoning, we would never have been able to translate an absurd act into an act that has a moral lesson. But literature, by force of its suggestive rhetoric, succeeds in opening the horizon of our moral world and in expanding it in places we had not imagined possible. Is this a positive expansion or, on the contrary, dangerous? This is another debate, both personal and generally philosophical.

PART TWO

The Moral Boundaries
of Psychology

I pointed out at the beginning of this book the increasingly powerful role played by psychological and psychoanalytical explanations in the mesh of literary commentaries. The more we are persuaded by these explanations to view the world and to understand the human soul through them and by them, the less are we able by ourselves to judge human activity morally. In the relationship between psychology and morality, however, psychology is becoming increasingly the more powerful. Here, I would like to single out three works that try to balance this relationship and to reinstate in moral judgment its value and its validity.

4

Morality Based on Guilt
or Morality Based on Sympathy

"THE WAY OUT" AND *NERVES*,
BY JOSEPH CHAIM BRENNER

In his informative book *To the Alley in Tiberias*,[1] Menahem Brinker describes the moral tension in J. C. Brenner's writing: "It is an undecided tension between a painstaking search for unchallenged moral certainties and the endless reproduction of life's problems that can be solved—if they can be solved at all in this way—only through improvisation that will always be carried out in accordance with circumstances and not in accordance with formula."

Two works by Brenner under discussion here have the moral issue at their core and demonstrate faithfully Menaham Brinker's observation with regard to moral certainties as against improvisation that is not carried out according to formula.[2] The discussion of the moral issue, as raised by "The Way Out" and *Nerves*, is important in itself, but especially intriguing is the difference in the moral concepts of the two works. As I said, the power of psychology in pushing aside the

1. Menahem Brinker, *To the Alley in Tiberias*, in Hebrew (Tel Aviv: Am Oved, 1990), 185.

2. I should like to recommend two excellent analyses of these two works: the first is of the story "The Way Out" in the book by Joseph Even, *J. C. Brenner's Art of Storytelling* (Jerusalem: Bialik Institute, 1977), 199–207; the second is of *Nerves* in Boaz Arpalli's book *The Negative Focus* (Tel Aviv: Hakibutz Heme'uhad and Katz Institute for Research into Hebrew Literature, 1992), 177–236.

moral debate is on the increase. Psychology offers an objective, non-judgmental explanation for human behavior so that even with problematic moral issues, psychological explanation and reasoning expel the stormy struggle between good and bad in favor of personal moods. Human behavior is explained in accordance with extenuation stemming from psychological structures or random situations and not in accordance with free intellectual choice between good and bad.

Thus, there is special interest in trying to show how an author with moral interest and foresight, both in his ideological concepts and his human concepts, tries to manifest the moral conflicts of two literary heroes in accordance with a principle that does not disregard the personal psychology of the hero but clearly tries to go beyond it in order to verify two types of moral behavior—the one that is activated by guilt and the other by sympathy. By doing so, Brenner imparts a greater advantage to a moral act that stems from identification than to a moral act that is born out of sense of guilt and duty.[3]

The plot of "The Way Out" takes place during the First World War after the British advance from the south into Palestine. After the conquest of Jerusalem and the southern part of Palestine, the British advance ceased for some reason, and the battlefront settled itself, frozen, between the British and the Turkish armies. The hero of the story, who is unnamed, is an old working-class teacher who lives on a farm near a settlement. At the sight of the refugees con-

3. In trying to confront these two stories, I am of course doing so on my own responsibility only. I am not trying to say that Brenner himself tried to do so. The novella *Nerves* was written in 1911, and the story "The Way Out" was written in 1919. The confrontation that I am conducting, while supplying a clear advantage to the element of sympathy over that of guilt, springs not only from the fact that both elements are very active in Brenner's works, but also from the fact that Brenner makes an obvious judgment with regard to the two characters in the two stories, the first destined to irony, the second to love.

gregating nearby, he goes into action and does his best to persuade people from the settlement to help, whether by supplying bread and water or by letting the refugees use the wagons so they can continue on their way. In the end, notwithstanding the old teacher's efforts and in spite of the harsh words he hurls at the settlement committee, he does not succeed in obtaining any real aid for the refugees and, especially, is unable to save the life of a baby girl who dies of starvation in her mother's arms. At the end of the story, the teacher hires the services of a hungry Turkish soldier to help him bury the dead baby. At the gravesite, however, he sprains his toe in one of the holes left in the ground after the cemetery fence was uprooted. This injury renders the teacher completely inactive. He returns to his hut and lies down on his bed, and the story ends with these words:

He lay alone in the dark room. He had tried bathing his toe in the cold water, but the throbbing pain had become unbearable and he was no longer able to move, not even to ease himself. Yet he felt strangely *relieved*, completely *absolved* of all his duties and needs.

He dimly made out the half-loaf of bread lying on the table amidst his books and soiled underwear, reminding him that he had not eaten a thing for three days, but the agonizing pain in his toe drove out all thoughts of food. Obeying some obscure impulse, he stretched out his hand to finger the bread, saw that it had gone stale and hard and was swept by remorse at not having taken the two whole loaves along with him. "What a great pity," he thought, "to let even a crust of bread go to waste right now . . ." His sorrow quickly passed, however, to make way for the sense of relief that flooded him. Ten minutes' walk away, the ruthless night spread unfriendly wings over the third batch of refugees. They had arrived unexpectedly that afternoon, his pupil had told him on their way to the farm, sixty-nine of them. But they were no longer his concern, he would not go to them, he was unable to go. He felt *relieved*.

I have laid special emphasis on the words *relieved* and *absolved*, one of which is even used to close the story. These two words may be placed alongside the story's title—"The Way Out"—and the author's ironic meaning becomes altogether clearer. There is no relief, after all, or absolution for the poor refugees who are filling the settlement, and there is certainly no way out of the agitated teacher's inadequacy. Thus, if the narrator is using such words, they should be taken to mean no more than an expression of irony that relates to our hero's emotional state and moral senses. After all, the old teacher in our story is a man of conscience, and just as he is able to demand, so also is he willing to give. With all his heart, he wants to help the refugees; he suffers with them and tries to coax the others into lending a helping hand. And yet, not only do all the goodness that flows from him, all the sympathy, and great sacrifice achieve no real significant effect, but they all even come to an end with a kind of strange and improper sense of relief and absolution, which totally contradicts the reality and the circumstances surrounding him.

The old teacher is a blatantly ideological person with a clear awareness of what has and what has not to be done. The fact that the author does not give him a name and insists on referring to him throughout as "the teacher" is no coincidence. He is a teacher who sees himself as a pedagogue, a guide, a man of morals, a preacher, and an interpreter—the ideal character of the do-gooder who adopts all the suffering of the world as if it is his own private suffering and is immediately filled with a sense of responsibility for alleviating this suffering. He wants to capture a broad area. His conscience is troubled by the entire refugee issue; he waits for them and goes into action as soon as they arrive. He tackles the members of the village action committee, censures them, and protests. There is no indication in the story that he enjoys his moral activity, and as a result he will never be able to feel that he has succeeded in it. He will always have the feeling that others are not doing as much as they can to solve problems. He treats the sufferers as if they are a single unit, making no distinction between the good, the truly needy, and the selfish among them—such as the red-haired Jew who takes over the wagons recruited by the settlement committee and piles them high with his own heavy boxes of merchandise instead of loading them with his fellow refugees. By paying too much attention to the general problem, the teacher overlooks the most severe case, the dying baby girl, who desperately needs his help. Had the teacher concentrated all his efforts on helping her rather than wasting his time and energy on useless argument with the members of the settlement committee, who are only deterred by his rebukes and do their best to avoid him, she might have survived that hectic day.

The old teacher has students, but the impression is that he is doing little to activate them. We learn of them only when one arrives after the teacher is injured to help him to his room. His moral authority is superficial. People appear to be turned off by his furious, tempestuous morality and tend not to follow him. The only person he manages to get in any way close to is the hungry Turkish soldier who helps him bury the little girl. Only with this pathetic soldier, with whom he shares no language, does he reach any kind of rapport, and in addition to a few coins, he suddenly lavishes the young man with gifts—a piece of cheese and a packet of cigarettes and, of course, the dead baby's cotton frock.

If we conduct a careful analysis of this short story within the narrow framework of the little we can draw from it, we shall see that the teacher's moral behavior is motivated principally by a sense of guilt, and it is this guilt that generates his commitment. It is the guilt of those who are well-off toward those whose fate has betrayed them. Although the teacher spends the night away from his own hut in order to identify with them and to be close to their refugee experience, this sympathy has no real value and is ultimately ineffective. He becomes more fractious and irritated as a result of his night of torture, and his rescue attempts are even less successful. Altogether, the old teacher seems less interested in helping out the refugees than in immersing himself in their situation and, by doing so, soothing a personal but somewhat immaterial sense of guilt at the inequality between himself and them.

Thus, it is easy enough to understand the teacher's feeling of relief and respite after his foot injury, which, like all injuries of this kind, is not merely accidental. He hurts himself in order to get rid of the heavy responsibility that forces him to feel guilty. The real problem is not the suffering of the refugees, but his own guilt toward suffering that is not his own. Thus, notwithstanding the moral commotion he induces and in spite of his tireless efforts to cause others to feel similar guilt pangs, the sum total of his moral activity is really rather meager. He quarrels with the people in his environment, and even the refugees themselves no longer have faith in him. Indeed, his activity is summed up and concluded in the burial of the baby girl he was unable to save, and the only beneficiary of all his energies is the hungry Turkish soldier, who is surprised to receive payment and gifts for his role in the burial.

With all due respect to social reformers and men of conscience, such as the old teacher, it is quite clear that the thread of their activity is limited, so that Brenner takes the liberty of describing them with obvious irony in his story "The Way Out," which in clear contradiction to its title offers no way out and no hope of a way out.

The novella *Nerves*, on the other hand, presents an infinitely more complex moral plot and a longer thread. Although its hero's psychological motivation is in itself problematic, its strength lies not only in his just and successful behavior in the existential situation in which he finds himself, but also in his ability to distinguish accurately and correctly between what is right and what is wrong in the world.

Nerves is built as a story within a story. The narrator of the first story is taking a walk with his friend one evening when he starts to tell the story of his immigration to Palestine. This friend is a complex intellectual character, with an interesting and original turn of thought that blends well with the naturalistic, slightly cruel description of his appearance: "an ordinary-looking man of about thirty with a set of strong sloping shoulders and a coarse featured, acne-studded face, who because he was ill had not gone to work this September day."

The conversation between the two friends is one of intimacy between two people who share the same intellectual codes so that as the friend begins to tell his story, it is quite clear that it is meant for someone who is also able to read between the lines.

The story is indeed complicated. It describes the adventures of a Ukrainian Jewish immigrant to New York who leaves after an eight-year stay that included work in a tailor's sweatshop. The life of poverty and hard work exhausts him, and he decides to start a new life in Palestine, not out of any naïve illusion that life would be easier there, but out of a hope of being able to grasp hold of something that has some kind of meaning, some kind of historical memory. But the move from America to Palestine—quite a novel route, not only in those days—was neither direct nor even easy, and it is the description of the shortcomings of this journey that stands at the center of the novella. The hero spends some time in an immigrants' hostel in London, where he shares a room with a recently arrived Jewish blacksmith from Bialystok. The man has tried to land in England with all his family, but they are refused entry by the immigration authorities, and he alone has been able to steal his way off the ship and onto dry land in the futile belief that he will manage to bring in his family once he is settled in England. But he ends up in that hostel, alongside other Jewish refugees, joking and laughing and playing all sorts of tricks, until finally discovering that his family has been returned by ship to Germany. He gets up one night, closes all the windows in his room, turns on the gas, and commits suicide.

Deeply shocked at the fate of this blacksmith and especially by the sharp and amazing transition from puerile horsing around to suicide, the storyteller continues on his way to Europe, and one day, just a few train stops away from Berlin, he happens across a Jewish family laden with luggage—a woman and her sister, accompanied by five daughters, the oldest of whom is eleven years old. The storyteller asks them where they are from, and although they tell him clearly that they are from Lithuania, from a town called Brest-Litovsk, he decides that they are actually from Bialystok, the same town from which that poor blacksmith had come to London before committing suicide, and insists in his imagination that the family before him is actually that man's lost family.

Once he has convinced himself that he has found the blacksmith's family, he attaches himself to them as a kind of guard-protector and helper in order to assist them in weathering their trials and tribulations.

'"But where are *you* coming from?'
'From London.'
'I'm from Yondon too,' beamed one of the smaller children from over the top of a bundle, while the sunny eyes of the eleven-year-old sister (because her eyes did have sunshine in them, that I must tell you, although it was sunshine that you didn't see at first, that you only noticed later) appraised me less harshly. You're laughing? But I tell you, she was as pretty as white satin. And what wild, lustrous hair! I'm sure that no one had washed it or combed it for weeks. . . .

'From Yondon,' said the younger one again.
As if I hadn't known all along!
So that now, neither the fact, which I soon discovered, that the woman had been a widow for years . . . nor that the reason for her deportation was not insufficient funds but a chronic eye condition . . . nor that her sister was turned back because a single woman could not enter England by herself . . . none of this made the slightest differ-

ence. My mind was made up: it was the same family! At once I hurried
to bring my bag from the car I had been sitting in. I felt almost en-
slaved to them, as though it were somehow my duty to serve them.
That's nerves for you!"

"A very Jewish case of them," I said sympathetically.

The Ukrainian Jew storyteller's adoption of this family seems extraordinary and special, a result of a strange illusion that stems from
a moral (yes, moral!) drive to help correct the tragedy of the pathetic
suicide in London—from a deep sympathy for the dead man that
brings the narrator to take his place and to offer patronage to the
poor deserted family even though he knows that it is not the same
family. The moral awakening of this neurotic man—who does not
deny that it is his strange capricious illusion to turn the family from
Brest-Litovsk into the family from Bialystok—is also accompanied
by a slight and somewhat perverted infatuation for the eleven-year-
old girl, who supports his moral behavior and makes it not only
strong and valid, but also effective. As opposed to the old teacher in
the story "The Way Out"—that professional do-gooder, with his too
general and rather abstract sense of morality, whose guilt complex
does not help him save even one small baby girl from death—this
neurotic, with his "nerves," succeeds, out of sympathy and devotion,
in leading this family to a safe haven in Palestine. And unlike that old
moralist, he saves the family and gives them financial assistance
without any fuss, with a quiet caution, and with an ironic undertone,
although the simple and poverty-stricken woman is suspicious and
tries at first to rid herself of this strange and foreign Jew who has decided to leech himself onto her and her family. Even after proving
several times the efficacy of his help, and even when he manages to
bring them to Palestine, still she seems unable to figure out the personality of her savior, who seems to her slightly out of his mind and
certainly not worthy of friendship and trust.

Thus, from that same motivation, that same strange adoption in which the Ukrainian Jew takes upon himself the job of the father who committed suicide, he helps the family on its way to Palestine. They lose contact after the meeting in Berlin, but renew it shortly afterward onboard the Palestine-bound ship from Trieste to Alexandria. It is very doubtful if without the help of our narrator, who is himself extremely short of funds, this family with its meager and miserable budget would have overcome all the problems involved in transferring from port to port and ship to ship and in entering Palestine although they have no entry permit. But out of the responsibility he had taken upon himself, he succeeds in getting the family through thick and thin to Palestine by maneuvering his way between the various Jewish go-betweens who offer their services. Here, in the confusion of Jewish go-betweens who attach themselves to unwary travelers and in two incidents that happen during his trouble-filled journey with "his family," as he defined them, the storyteller discovers a simple but deep and essential moral truth. One incident involves the sadistic duplicity of a wicked and cunning Jewish Egyptian go-between who takes advantage of the voyagers' ignorance in order to trick them out of their money, and the second offers a complete contrast in the form of another Jewish Egyptian go-between who is good-hearted and sincere, who not only gives them real assistance during an important part of their journey, but actually empties his own pockets on behalf of complete strangers.

The reader should also bear in mind the storyteller's existential starting point—a worldview that held that everything is worthless, and that against the certainty and infinity of inevitable death, every definition and every determination in the human world are dwarfed. With these thoughts, the storyteller sets off on his journey from America, aware that there is no real difference between sewing buttons in New York and picking oranges in Palestine, yet he decides, after all, to go to Palestine for reasons not quite clear even to himself.

On the way, when he comes across different kinds of moral behavior in people—especially the two Jews in Egypt, the crook and the righteous man—he understands that although in the end everything is one with respect to death, so long as man lives, he must distinguish between good and bad. He must fill his life with moral content, no matter what. I believe this is the main moral conclusion of the story.

Thus, in the midst of the journey's trials and tribulations, the story-teller—in his adopted role of father to the family—discovers, in a way that is so much more sober and adult than that of the old man in "The Way Out," the real character of the moral world. Through the depth of personal sympathy for the objects of his kindness, he discovers the bitter truth—that there are people who cheat, harm, and do evil deeds not because they are unaware of what is good and right, but because they have a genuine desire to do evil. In other words, not only is evil a dearth of goodness; it is evil for the sake of evil. Genuine evil. Just as, in contradiction, goodness is genuine goodness.

He makes this discovery during the ordeals of the journey, having to cope with immigration and customs authorities, with travel tickets, with wagon owners, and then to struggle for entry permits to Palestine. These matters are ostensibly minor, but for helpless and penniless travelers, they are dramatic and potentially fateful. And because those involved in these confrontations are Jewish go-betweens—some of them men of goodwill, with a genuine desire to help, and others wicked and corrupt, who take advantage of the plight of the refugees in order to make more money at their expense—the story distinguishes clearly and unequivocally between good and bad. In the commotion of the port of Alexandria and at the railway station in Cairo and Port Said, in the struggle for entry in Jaffa port and then in Haifa—in all these situations and their degrading bureaucracy, our storyteller, with his finely tuned senses, who has undertaken the pathetic and comic responsibility for this wandering family, arrives at a profound moral revelation, which he defines thus:

"I myself, once I had regained my composure, fetched a bit of water, washed the sweat from my hands and face, peeled myself an or-
ange, took a piece of bread to go with it, and made a brave attempt to
eat. (Not that I was hungry, although I hadn't tasted a single thing all
day.) Yet with the first bite I took I was overcome with dread all over
again at the contrast between the two men whom we had met by
accident that day, the dread of the contrast between 'no good'
and 'good.' . . . No, I don't mean good and evil in relation to me or
the effect it had on me, or on that wreck of a woman with her five
children who was the symbol of Jewish homelessness and misfortune.
. . . What I mean is . . . good and evil, and all that they imply, in
themselves. . . . Good and evil as two different worlds, two essences
. . . with an infinite abyss between them. Good lord, how infinite it
was! And how tragic human life was, how hard, how hard it was to
live!

The slice of bread stuck in my throat, and the tears began to come
nonstop. They were hysterical, those tears, yet at the same time quiet
and unobtrusive. Some Arabs, on their way to the Holy Sepulchre,
stared at me with the knowledge that I was a sufferer in life, and that
Allah had not been kind to me."

This is not the last time in this novella that our hero bursts into
tears. Nor is it the last time that he is shaken so profoundly into
awareness by the moral experience he is encountering. But unlike
the old teacher in "The Way Out"—who feels a grim, dissatisfied
anger and who escapes from his futile, inefficient strivings and
from the obligations imposed on him by guilt by lying down in his
moldy, un-made-up bed to wallow in masochistic pleasure at the
pain in his big toe—the hero of *Nerves* undergoes a powerful
cathartic process of cleansing and understanding. He does not lose
spirit in face of all the hardships; on the contrary, he draws strength
and life from the moral act and the moral awareness that he has
achieved.

"So in the end I gave the remaining five francs to the woman 'for a rainy day' and kept the leftover sous for myself. My eleven-year-old darling took her frozen hands out of the sleeves in which she had been keeping them and threw me a special look. She stuck her hands back into her sleeves, but her look gave me strength . . . so that again, for all the hopelessness of the situation, for all its radical sorrow, it seemed to me that it was definitely worth living and that there were things worth living for. . . . Yes, that it was actually pleasant to be alive. This phantasmal notion came and went in a moment, but as long as that moment lasted it made sense. It too of course could not have withstood the scalpel of the intellect, that icicle of the consciousness of reality as it is, not to mention the nothingness that comes after as it is. . . . Yet at that moment I wanted to cry out with all my being: Yes! Yes! Yes!"

This is a description of a powerful experience, and our hero receives wonderful and profound compensation for his good deed, which was motivated by a personal, private, and anonymous sympathy—compensation that is greater and richer than any possible expression of thanks on the part of the widowed mother of the family, who, until the last moment, remains remote and skeptical toward him. This, then, is the description of their leave taking, after they have succeeded in landing in Haifa, and the hero is overcome with tears of joy.

" 'But look how this young man can't stop crying!' said the second hotelkeeper, half marveling at me, half making fun. 'Ai, ai, ai!' he mimicked. 'Fool, what is there to cry about?'

I suppose the way I must have looked just then more than justified his addressing me in such affectionate terms.

'Oy,' I whimpered like a naughty child in front of them. 'We're in Palestine.'

'So much the better then, why cry?' persisted the hotelkeeper.

The bystanders broke into smiles. 'He's crying for joy . . . for joy that he's here.'

'He cries easily,' sniffed the woman with a shake of her head. A last drop hung from the tip of her nose; all else appeared already to have evaporated, and she was once again the person she had always been.

I wiped away my own tears . . . why attempt to deny it? A warm trickle of happiness filtered through me as I looked now at my little friend, who refused to budge from my side, now at the shore. And each time I looked at her—who knew what lay in store for her?— I understood again what I had already realized that morning, that is . . . that as long as we are alive . . . whatever happens to us does make a difference, it does . . . and that the unbridgeable abyss between the two men we had encountered the day before in Alexandria and Port Said was present also in our two comings ashore."

The moral act that stems from guilt might be fine, but in the final analysis, because it aims at satisfying the needs of the giver rather than those of the receiver, the thread of its duration is short. Activity that stems from sympathy, that takes on the other as if he or she were a member of the giver's family, might be unruly and undisciplined, but in the end, the thread of its duration is longer and stronger, and its moral definition is also truer. Thus, the advantage of the hero with "nerves" over the old teacher from "The Way Out" does not stem from the fact that the former succeeds in his mission and the latter does not, but rather from the fact that if the hero in *Nerves* had sustained any injury—for example as happened to the old teacher— and his injury had prevented him from continuing his help to his adopted family, he would not have felt relieved or absolved. He would have felt pain and fear and deep frustration for not being able to help his "family."

The author of the two stories has succeeded in presenting moral dilemmas that have a universal significance, while remaining within the ideological turmoil involved in dealing with questions on the

Jewish nation and on Zionism, and in describing renewed Jewish life in the prestate of Israel Palestine. Although the behavior of the two heroes in the two stories results from their individual personalities and motivations, the difference between the two basic principles that guide them is what ultimately makes the difference between success and failure under similar circumstances.

There is no doubt that these two stories do not end only on the personal level of two dissimilar personalities. Rather, they have repercussions on much broader public activity. But such repercussions are beyond the boundaries of the debate that we have defined for this book.

♣ 5 ♣

The Terrible Power of a Minor Guilt

THE ETERNAL HUSBAND,
BY FYODOR DOSTOYEVSKY

Let us go to the final chapter, to the end of this short novel, *The Eternal Husband,* by Dostoyevsky. We are in a country railway station somewhere in the depths of Russia, a couple of years after the stormy events related in the novel, which took place—in the way of Dostoyevsky's novels—over a brief but intense period of several weeks. The two heroes meet by chance. Pavel Pavlovitch, the eternal husband, is taking his new young wife to his estate, together with his wife's new lover, while Velchaninov is on his way to a meeting with a lady (married, no doubt) who has captured his romantic interest. In other words, the situation at the basis of the conflict that burst forth with such force on the arrival of the widowed eternal husband in Petersburg exists once again and is moving along according to the same pattern. The heroes have both reverted to their evil ways.

Pavel Pavlovitch and Velchaninov meet suddenly during a brief stopover on the train journey and strike up a conversation, at the end of which Velchaninov extends his hand in friendship. This hand is still mutilated, a reminder of Pavlovitch's attempt to murder the sick Velchaninov, who had needed enormous effort to ward off his assailant. But Pavel Pavlovitch refuses to take the outstretched hand. Velchaninov indicates the deep scar and says to Pavlovitch:

74

"If I—*I* hold out this hand to you," showing the palm of his left hand, where a big scar from the cut was still distinct, "you certainly might take it!" he whispered, with pale and trembling lips.

Pavel Pavlovitch, too, turned pale, and his lips trembled too; a convulsive quiver ran over his face.

"And Liza?" he murmured in a rapid whisper, and suddenly his lips, his cheeks and his chin began to twitch and tears gushed from his eyes.

Velchaninov stood before him stupefied.

Although Pavlovitch himself, through wicked abuse and alienation, caused the death of Liza, fruit of Velchaninov's adulterous affair with Pavlovitch's now deceased wife, he still has the impertinence to mention the dead girl as a moral reason to refuse the handshake of the man who is actually his victim. Velchaninov, however, does not strike out against the abuser and murderer, but stands, rooted to the spot, proving—most intensely—the power of a minor guilt, until the reader is able if not to sympathize with (and indeed it is very difficult to do so), then at least to *understand* the eternal husband's refusal to make peace with his wife's lover at the end of the story.

If I were obliged to sum up in a few sentences the dynamics of the moral dialogue in this powerful and intense novel, I believe I would do so thus: a rich, complex, and persuasive alliance of psychological reasoning is laid out here that perfectly explains the heroes' behavior and positions each of them in his right place with regard to his relations with his counterparts. Against this alliance there stands a moral guilt, which by any criteria cannot be considered a grave guilt. Nonetheless, none of the complex psychological rationales has the ability to cancel out the power of that guilt, either in the heart of the victim, who demands revenge, or in the heart of the assailant, who is prepared to cooperate with the revenge planned against him, even if it leads to extreme, even criminal acts. For this reason, I have defined the debate on the moral map of this piece of literature as "the terrible power of a minor guilt."

Before us, therefore, is an illuminating example of nineteenth-century literature that clearly prefers to impart stronger existential power to moral considerations than to psychological rationalizations and "platitudes." As far as I am concerned, this preference is a highly inspiring example for readers of twentieth-century literature for whom psychology has achieved so dominant a position both in real life and in literature.

The hero of this novel is Velchaninov, a forty-year-old bachelor, handsome and popular among the ladies, who has courted and seduced many women, many of them married. Nine years previously, Velchaninov was a guest in the home of Pavel Pavlovitch, where he fell deeply in love with Pavel's wife, Natalya Vassilyevna. It was she who, to a great extent, initiated the affair with her husband's guest. The affair continued for a full year, until she broke it off. Natalya is far from being depicted as a naïve romantic in the style of other literary love stories that involve highly erotic men and bored provincial wives.

> She was not exactly pretty; perhaps she was actually plain. She was twenty-eight when Velchaninov first knew her. Though not altogether beautiful, her face was sometimes charmingly animated, but her eyes were not pretty: there was something like an excess of determination in them. She was very thin. On the intellectual side she had not been well educated; her keen intelligence was unmistakable, though she was one-sided in her ideas. Her manners were those of a provincial lady and at the same time, it is true, she had a great deal of tact; she had artistic taste, but showed it principally in knowing how to dress. In character she was resolute and domineering; she could never make up her mind to compromise in anything: it was all, or

nothing. In difficult positions her firmness and stoicism were amazing. She was capable of generosity and at the same time would be utterly unjust. To argue with that lady was impossible: "twice two makes four" meant nothing to her. She never thought herself wrong or to blame in anything. Her continual deception of her husband and the perfidies beyond number which she practised upon him did not weigh on her in the least. But, to quote Velchaninov's own comparison, she was like the "Madonna of the Flagellants," who believes implicitly herself that she is the mother of God—so Natalya Vassilyevna believed implicitly in everything she did. She was faithful to her lover, but only as long as he did not bore her. She was fond of tormenting her lover, but she liked making up for it too. She was of a passionate cruel and sensual type. She hated depravity and condemned it with exaggerated severity and—was herself depraved.

This, then, was the woman with whom Velchaninov committed adultery. The husband, according to Dostoyevsky's detailed description and in the way of many cuckolded men, actually invited the infidelity into his home, strangely, yet deliberately ignoring the lover's presence. Velchaninov was not Pavlovitch's wife's first lover, nor was he the last. He was replaced by Bugaotov (although there was still another one in between, a young artillery officer whom Pavlovitch's wife used as an excuse to get rid of Velchaninov), whose stormy five-year affair with Pavlovitch's wife was conducted without her husband having so much as an inkling of what was going on behind his back.

The wife was therefore a chronic adulteress, obsessive, with a husband who was dying to be cuckolded and who invited and encouraged the lovers to visit his home. If we dare suppose that this same Natalya Vassilyevna, who has just been described in great detail, was no ordinary woman, then at the end of his novel, Dostoyevsky makes a point of informing us that the husband's reconciliation to his wife's peccadilloes right under his nose stemmed not from any special qualities or powers in the wife, but from her coldness toward her spouse, who is referred to as the "eternal husband." Pavel Pavlovitch thrives on the constant presence of a lover. At the end of the story, his new young wife also has in tow a lover, whom her husband, as usual, takes the trouble to nurture and encourage, although as always with a kind of "naïveté" and a stubborn "disregard," despite his rich experience in "finding" lovers in his home.

The question, therefore, is what has morality got to do with this triangle: an actively unfaithful wife, a husband whose psyche requires that he be betrayed by his wife, and an unmarried lover, with much experience and an excellent reputation in adultery? What is the point of moral judgment in the case of such drives, perversions, and frivolities? Dostoyevsky nevertheless does manage to introduce an element of morality, with a power that is destructive in the extreme, via a fourth character, who has absolutely no connection with or responsibility for the psychological complexity that binds the story's three protagonists.

It appears that Natalya Vassilyevna's love affair with Velchaninov did not end without residue, and the woman found herself pregnant, which is the reason why she decided to end suddenly her relationship with Velchaninov, who was thrown out of the house without knowing the real (and apparently not the only) reason for the breakup. A daughter was born, Liza, with whom Pavel Pavlovitch was inordinately happy, following many years of childlessness. For nine years he has no idea, of course, that Liza is not his child, but after Natalya's sudden death, he discovers a number of letters that she had not had time to destroy, including those written to her by lovers and those she had written but not sent to lovers. Among the letters is an unsent one to Velchaninov, in which Natalya Vassilyevna informs him that she is expecting his child.

After his wife's death, therefore, the widowed "eternal husband" arrives in Petersburg like some dark avenging spirit, a black crepe—

bedecked hat on his head. Just as he had been naïve, reconciled, and relaxed in his ignorance of the betrayals and adulteries conducted in his home by his wife's guests, so is he cruel and uninhibited in his revenge now that her activity has become known to him. Logically, his sudden bereavement should have reduced the power of his revenge; his faithless wife, the object of his love, is no longer alive, and there is no longer reason to wreak revenge on her lovers. When the betrayed eternal husband is left without the wife whom he so admired and loved, he becomes a missile whose control mechanism has gone haywire and starts to operate on its own destructive and unbridled energy. Thus, Pavel Pavlovitch decides to settle accounts with all those who had previously abused his trust. First of all, he takes great pleasure in the death throes of the five-year-long lover, Bugaotov. He then turns to Velchaninov, taking a special gift to him, poor little Liza, whom, after learning that he is not her father, he had decided to torture horribly before throwing her upon her real father. He lives with her in a dubious and miserable boarding house, goes on wild rampages involving alcohol and brothels, and leaves her trapped in the room, dissolving in her fears for her beloved father, the only person left to her in the world. In no time at all, Pavel Pavlovitch's great love for his daughter is consumed in the fire of revenge for the lover who betrayed his trust, and he torments the girl with such utter cruelty as to altogether upset her mind and health until she declines completely.

From a moral point of view, Pavel Pavlovitch's journey of revenge is built on a single element—betrayal, and Velchaninov's betrayal is especially bitter because Pavel Pavlovitch revered Velchaninov:

> "I loved you, Alexey Ivanovitch," Pavel Pavlovitch articulated, as though he had suddenly made up his mind to speak, "and all that year at T——I loved you. You did not notice it," he went on, in a voice that quivered, to Velchaninov's positive horror; "I was too insignifi-

cant, compared with you, to let you see it. And there was no need, indeed, perhaps. And I've thought of you all these nine years, because
there has never been another year in my life like that one" (Pavel
Pavlovitch's eyes began to glisten). "I remembered many of your
phrases and sayings, your thoughts. I always thought of you as a man
with a passion for every noble feeling, a man of education, of the
highest education and of ideas: 'Great ideas spring not so much from
noble intelligence as from noble feeling.' You said that yourself; perhaps you've forgotten it, but I remembered it. I always looked on you,
therefore, as a man of noble feeling . . . and therefore believed in
you—in spite of anything."

Pavel Pavlovitch delivers this emotional speech several hours before
he attempts to murder the object of his love and admiration. Perhaps
it is because the love and trust were so great that the sense of disap-
pointment and revenge are equally intense.

The guiding principle in *The Eternal Husband* is the obvious and outspoken disproportion between the severity of the moral guilt and the
emotional and moral effect it engenders. In other words, there are injustices that by all moral criteria will not be considered severe and
might even appear flippant, not only in comparison with much more
serious crimes, but also because these unjust acts can be rationalized
psychologically and sociologically in a way that can explain and
even justify their existence. And yet, these acts can arouse such furious and morally destructive reactions.

In *The Eternal Husband*, Dostoyevsky succeeds in supplying a psychological explanation for the moral flavor of the disproportionate
and violent reaction on the part of a man who defines himself as the
injured party. But he also succeeds—and here is the secret of this
novel's uniqueness—in revealing the psychological texture of the
other side, the offender and betrayer, who cooperates with the vic-

tim, whether knowingly or not, in a most destructive manner that very nearly brings about his own murder.

Pavel Pavlovitch appears in Velchaninov's life at a time when the latter is suffering deep depression and is at odds with the world. The official reason for this state of affairs is a court case regarding an inheritance in which his involvement is deeper than necessary, and in an attempt to reach an agreement, he has complicated things further and aroused his lawyer's concern. This case, to which Dostoyevsky attaches little real significance, causes Velchaninov to retire temporarily from society, to neglect himself, and to fall into a bad lifestyle. When Pavel Pavlovitch arrives in town, he meets a man who is troubled, angry, and sick, whose legal complications exaggerate his sense of moral guilt. The love affairs of this promiscuous bachelor have caused trouble not only for Pavel Pavlovitch's wife, but for other married women as well.

And thus Velchaninov explains his mood to his friend Claudia Petrovnia, in whose pleasant, child-filled home he tries to find shelter for Liza, who is being tormented by a man who has discovered that he is no longer her father:

> "Don't shake your head and don't blame me; I blame myself and have blamed myself, for the whole affair, long ago, long ago! . . . You see, I was so certain he knew when I was there this morning that I compromised myself before him. Would you believe it, I felt so wretched and ashamed at having met him so rudely yesterday (I will tell you about it fully afterwards). He came to me yesterday from an irresistible, malicious desire to let me know that he knew of the wrong done him, and knew who had done it; that was the whole reason of his stupid visit when he was drunk. But that was so natural on his part! He simply came to work off his resentment! I was altogether too hasty with him this morning and yesterday! Careless—stupid! I betrayed myself to him. Why did he turn up at a moment when I was upset? I tell you he's even been tormenting Liza, tormenting the child,

and probably that, too, was to work off his resentment—to vent his malice if only on the child! Yes, he is spiteful—insignificant as he is, yet he is spiteful; very much so indeed. In himself he is no more than a buffoon, though God knows, in old days he seemed to be a very decent fellow within his limits—it's so natural that he should be going to the dogs! One must look at it from a Christian point of view! And you know, my dear, my best of friends, I want to be utterly different to him; I want to be kind to him. That would be really a 'good deed' on my part. For, you know, after all, I have wronged him! Listen, you know there's something else I must tell you. On one occasion in T——I was in want of four thousand roubles, and he lent me the money on the spot, with no security, and showed genuine pleasure at being of use to me; and, do you know, I took it then, I took it from his hands. I borrowed money from him, do you understand, as a friend!"

Velchaninov is already getting himself ready to express his guilt to Pavel Pavlovitch, without even conceiving the power and depth of the fury harboring in the heart of the man in the crepe-bedecked hat. From here on, by strength of this small and specific minor guilt and in a desire to do "a good deed," he will get into deeper and deeper trouble, until virtually succumbing to that guilt completely. Despite the fact that the woman with whom he had a love affair was an out-and-out adulteress who changed lovers at the drop of a hat—a woman who concealed from him the fact of her pregnancy and banished him from her home suddenly and without so much as an explanation, a woman whose husband needed her to have lovers and made sure to welcome them into his home—his sense of guilt is still powerful. If we were to weigh this particular act of adultery on its own, it would be easy to find many reasons to be lenient in our judgment of Velchaninov's behavior. But Velchaninov is positively dying to be guilty, and his guilt leads him to cooperate with his accuser, who is totally carried away with his passion for revenge. Although he sees how Pavel Pavlovitch torments the little girl—Velchaninov's own daughter—and is actually responsible for her death by refusing to visit her on her deathbed, he does not break off relations with the "scoundrel." After the girl's funeral (which Pavel Pavlovitch does not attend), Velchaninov is even willing to cooperate with him in an attempt at matchmaking, pairing off the elderly widower with a fifteen-year-old girl. He takes him to the girl's home, advises him on the kind of jewelry to buy the young bride, and musters all his charm and experience with the ladies in order to help the revolting "bridegroom," who is so eager to make inroads with the family of the terrified little "Lolita."

Moreover, in spite of Pavel Pavlovitch's terrible cruelty toward his daughter and his nasty and sick attempts to exploit the poverty of a decent family with too many daughters by getting himself hitched up with a young schoolgirl, the power of Velchaninov's guilt urges him to maintain contact with this man who is growing more and more obnoxious by the moment. He invites Pavel Pavlovitch into his home and even allows him to confuse and deceive him, until he falls ill. At first, Pavel Pavlovitch nurses the sick Velchaninov and lies beside him to protect him in his illness, but then one night he gets up to slaughter the sick man with a knife. Velchaninov fortunately manages to muster his last strength to push off his assailant; otherwise, his end would have been bitter indeed.

But if it seems to us that here Velchaninov is released from the suffocating yoke of his guilt and from his sick interaction with the eternal husband—the description of the struggle with the murderer and of the recovery that follows it shows us that Velchaninov must regain both physical and emotional health—we might find ourselves surprised once again. As in life, so in novels by Dostoyevsky, nothing is absolute, final. Despite Velchaninov's feeling of freedom and relief after warding off the murderer and then sending him on his way, there is no promise that the strange pattern of this relationship will not be repeated. Man's nature is stronger than his wisdom, and the moral element is a highly powerful consideration in his neurotic complexity.

The epilogue, in which the two heroes meet two years later, reveals that they are both prepared to repeat the mistakes of the past. The eternal husband has attached himself once again to a younger woman, who is trailed by the obligatory lover, and Velchaninov, the eternal unmarried lover, is still searching for an extramarital romantic adventure with a married woman. When he sets his eyes on Pavel Pavlovitch's pretty young wife, he is tempted for a moment to make his way to his adversary's home and perhaps to relive history, with all its attendant horror and tragedy.

In spite of all the horrible things that Velchaninov has endured at the hands of Pavel Pavlovitch, he is still not about to discredit him. Empowered terribly by the minor guilt of betrayal he bears in his heart toward this ridiculous and obnoxious man, this foolish and depraved man, Velchaninov, extends his scarred hand in peace. But it is Pavel Pavlovitch who refuses to accept the outstretched hand because the terrible power of his fury at the injustice caused him by his dead wife's lover still supersedes the appalling acts he perpetrated in revenge. Because he senses his victim's basic feeling of guilt, he denies him the chance to make peace.

The moral consideration, the moral pain, and the moral affront are stronger than any reason and explanation supplied by psychology books, be they ever so reliable and stable. Morality dodges the sheath of psychology and takes for itself the status of leader in driving the plot and the characters of this novel.

In a certain sense, it would appear today that only literature is able to free itself somewhat from the bonds of relative sociological, psychologistic, political, and cultural discourse that has completely taken over control of all matters of morality to such an extent that one can no longer present a moral judgment without having to offer a thousand rationalizations. Modern literature is mostly too subservient to psychology, and even when it does not enter into the fund of purposes and reasons, and decides to make do with presenting "given" situations only, the reader, who is well versed in psychological discourse, is able to make up for the lack by using his or her power of imagination and thought: in the modern era, there is no such thing as pure evil for the sake of it; there is no wickedness just for the sake of it. Behind evil and wickedness, there always lurk explanations and reservations. Thus, how good it is that we can still sometimes come across a novel written by a brilliant nineteenth-century author who, despite the rich sophistication and psychological complexity of his characters, is able to shake both them and us the readers to the core by force of a simple and minor moral guilt, and by doing so to teach—who knows—modern literature not to relinquish too easily the right to place moral issues at the top of literary creativity.

PART THREE

The Moral Responsibility
of Denial Processes

What is the extent of man's moral responsibility? Philosophers and lawyers have grappled often with this weighty issue. Does man's moral responsibility for good or bad touch only on things that he does or on things that he does not do as well? A person who knew about a murder that was about to be committed and did nothing to prevent it is considered guilty by law and certainly despicable morally because knowledge, too, has moral weight. If a person knows of an imminent crime, he or she bears the moral responsibility to make use of that knowledge. But moral discussions are far-reaching and also take into consideration the fact that a person could have known, but refused to know. This area is a very foggy, but real—containing the blurred borders between knowledge and ignorance, the moral responsibility of denial processes, and the emotional fiber between the conscious and the subconscious. Using fine analytical tools, lawyers, psychologists, and analysts constantly try to come to terms with this area. All the more reason, therefore, for readers and literary critics to make similar analyses of written texts that deal often with

denial processes, release, and insight of human awareness. I would
like to refer this moral debate to two classical literary texts that actu-
alize, each in its own original way, the moral responsibility of denial
processes: William Faulkner's "A Rose for Emily" and S. Y. Agnon's
In the Prime of Her Life.

⚜ 6 ⚜

Society Pays Homage to a Murderess
with a Freshly Cut Rose

"A ROSE FOR EMILY,"
BY WILLIAM FAULKNER

Let us open, as usual with the final scene of this story, a scene that descends upon the reader with great force.[1]

> The violence of breaking down the door seemed to fill this room with pervading dust. A thin, acrid pall as of the tomb seemed to lie everywhere upon this room decked and furnished as for a bridal: upon the valence curtains of faded rose color, upon the rose shaded lights, upon the dressing table, upon the delicate array of crystal and the man's toilet things backed with tarnished silver, silver so tarnished that the monogram was obscured. Among them lay a collar and tie, as if they had just been removed, which, lifted, left upon the surface a pale crescent in the dust. Upon a chair hung the suit, carefully folded; beneath it the two mute shoes and the discarded socks.
> The man himself lay in the bed.
> For a long while we stood there, looking down at the profound and fleshless grin. The body had apparently once lain in the attitude of an embrace, but now the long sleep that outlasts love, that con-

---

1. I was helped in this discussion on Faulkner by two papers. The first is Mena-hem Perry's paper, published in Hebrew in *Hasafrut* 28 (April 1979): 64–66. The second is Cleanth Brooks and Robert Penn Warren, *Understanding Fiction* 2d ed. (New York: Appleton-Century-Crofts, 1959), the chapter devoted to this story.

quers even the grimace of love, had cuckolded him. What was left of him, rotted beneath what was left of the night-shirt, had become inextricable from the bed in which he lay; and upon him and upon the pillow beside him lay that even coating of the patient and biding dust.

Then we noticed that in the second pillow was the indentation of a head. One of us lifted something from it, and leaning forward, that faint and invisible dust dry and acrid in the nostrils, we saw a long strand of iron-gray hair.

Not only does it become apparent that Homer Barron, the long-lost lover, had been poisoned by Miss Emily and that his body had lain for forty years in the room on the second floor of her house, but it is equally clear that Miss Emily lay down each night beside him throughout all those years.

These shocking facts lend the story an aspect that is at once fantastic and profound. However, when we calm down somewhat from the shock of the story's ending, we ask ourselves, as readers, whether the withholding of this information during the course of the story had any substantially profound reason or whether it was mere manipulation on the part of the narrator, who was hoping in this way to keep us in suspense. Would the story have lost any of its flavor had information on the murder and perhaps also the fact of the lady's habit of lying down next to the corpse been disclosed somewhere near the beginning of the story?

If we go back and read the story from start to finish, already in possession of the information we received at its end, we are surprised to notice that the flavor of the story is not dulled; on the contrary, it has become richer, sharper, and fuller bodied. We understand it better now that we can fill in and take up some of the hints that we had previously passed over.

If we return to the story a third time, we will realize that a whole new system of reasons justifies the first part of the amazing ending. As we reread the story, the second climax sheds new light on Miss Emily's personality and on the special interaction she had with the inhabitants of the township.

After all, the double climax that lands on us at the end of the story is not a release of tension that needs explaining. This is not a detective story in the course of which we were asking ourselves who the murderer is or where the body is hidden because we did not really guess that there had been a murder, nor did we search for a missing corpse. Nonetheless, the end, with both its surprises, is not dropped on the story from outside; it grows from within, and it is believable and convincing. Everything that bothered us about this story could only have been deciphered in this way. In other words, the information here is foreseeable and very reliable, but also surprising and shocking. How can these two conflicting descriptions combine?

It is my opinion that the combination is possible only if we say that our awareness of details was repressed, hidden in our subconscious. On the one hand, we are amazed at the discovery, but on the other, we feel that the details were indeed within us, although they were repressed. When we become aware of things that were concealed in our subconscious, we undergo simultaneously that same special blend of complete surprise and great familiarity.

This, therefore, is the story's emotional movement. Saving the amazing details to the very end of the story is not done for the purpose of determining the author's superiority over his readers. Faulkner put off revealing the facts to the end of the story in order to create in the reader a deeper compatibility with the townsfolk in discovering what they have repressed as they enter or burst into their own subconscious after Miss Emily's death.

We were already aware earlier on of a room on the second floor that no one had seen for forty years and that needed bursting into. In that case, there was a deeper but repressed knowledge of this room in which the murdered man lay for forty years. Had the information of the murder been supplied to us earlier over the heads of the townsfolk, we would have been unable to be with them at this important moment, which is the focal point of the story. This story is not, after all, about Miss Emily, but rather about the relationship between her and the townsfolk.

In short stories, there is a tradition of using amazing points to turn a story upside down at the end, as if saying to the reader, "Whatever you know up to now is untrue"—for example, in Guy de Maupassant's famous story "The Necklace." There are also stories, however—such as Faulkner's—that tell their readers, "Whatever you knew until now is of more significance than you thought."

If in Albert Camus's story "The Guest" we found nothing that could explain Daru's decision not to hand in the Arab, here in this instance the situation is completely opposite. Each detail in the story, whether on a personal family level or on a social and even political level, lends additional back-up to the astonishing finale, both in its first part, the murder, and in its second part, the evidence of the old woman lying next to the corpse of the murdered lover.

It is possible in the story to locate five layers of explanation for Miss Emily's behavior. The first is connected to Miss Emily's personality and to her family's pathological background; the second is connected to the special relationship she shared with her father; the third is tied to Homer Barron and his relationship with her; the fourth, and most important, is connected to the social fiber within the township; and the fifth goes way back to the broad political situation of the U.S. Civil War. It is quite fascinating and amazing that so many levels of significance can be brought together in one short story.

Emily herself is described as being strange, if we are to be polite, and disturbed, if we are to be more accurate. People in town remembered how old lady Wyatt, her great aunt, had gone completely crazy at last. Miss Emily's strangeness becomes quite obvious after her father dies, when she tries to deny his death and refuses the municipal authorities permission to take the body away for burial.

The most powerful expressions of Miss Emily's disturbed nature are her necrophilia and her failure to distinguish between the living and the dead—or, more accurately, her nonacceptance of death. It is not possible to tell whether this nonacceptance stems from insanity or from cold calculation. For example, at the beginning of the story, she is "visited by a deputation of town dignitaries trying to get her to pay her taxes, and she refers them to Colonel Sartoris (who had been dead for almost ten years), who, or so she reckoned, had exempted her father from paying taxes."

Here, too, like the time she refuses to release her father's body for burial, it is not only uncompromising madness that is at work, but something more mercenary, perhaps an unwillingness to pay taxes or a desire to take revenge on her father for his injustice toward her. We must not, therefore, get carried away in seeing Miss Emily as no more than a crazy woman. Had she really been so, it would be more difficult for us to identify with her behavior and to understand the tragic trap into which she had maneuvered herself in her relations with the townsfolk. The pathological background of her personality appears in the story only as a fine undercoat, over which different layers of meaning are piled. As we shall see later, her necrophilic tendencies and her refusal to see the dead as dead lend her special power and importance in the eyes of the society of which she is a part.

The second level—the one that is clearer with regard to the double ending (the murder and the devoted proximity to the murdered man's corpse)—is tied to the special relationship Miss Emily had with her father. Faulkner makes no mention whatsoever of Miss Emily's mother, who probably either disappeared or died when Emily was very young. On the other hand, he does use terse, sharp, and extremely clear sentences to describe her relationship with her father.

> Miss Emily a slender figure in white in the background, her father a spraddled silhouette in the foreground, his back to her and clutching a horsewhip, the two of them framed by the back-flung front door. So when she got to be thirty and was still single, we were not pleased exactly, but vindicated; with insanity in the family she wouldn't have turned down all of her chances if they had really materialized.
>
> When her father died, it got about that the house was all that was left to her; and in a way people were glad. At last they could pity Miss Emily. Being left alone, and a pauper, she had become humanized. Now she too would know the old thrill and the old despair of a penny more or less.
>
> The day after his death all the ladies prepared to call at the house and offer condolence and aid, as is our custom. Miss Emily met them at the door, dressed as usual and with no trace of grief on her face. She told them that her father was not dead. She did that for three days, with the ministers calling on her, and the doctors, trying to persuade her to let them dispose of the body. Just as they were about to resort to law and force, she broke down, and they buried her father quickly.

Miss Emily's father is a spraddled silhouette in the foreground, his back to her and a horsewhip clutched in his hand, probably to drive away all potential suitors for his daughter, whom he wanted to keep for himself. An oedipal relationship if ever there was one, full of tension and powerful mutual attraction, coupled, of course, with much animosity. Indeed, an attempt to prevent the burial of her dead father and to remain closeted in the house with the corpse is something that has in it overwhelming attraction, but also resentment and revenge.

It thus stands to reason that after her father's death, Miss Emily would try to find a similar recipe for a relationship. It could almost be said that Homer Barron is a kind of clone of Miss Emily's father: arrogant, his hat cocked and a cigar in his teeth, reins and whip in a yellow glove, a father figure to whom she is fiercely attracted, but at the same time one who is forbidden to her by dint of the laws of incest. So it's no wonder that she repeats her unsuccessful experience with her father. In other words, only by having the father figure lie dead in bed can the taboo of lying with the father be lifted.

A third level explains the amazing double ending of the story, tied to the two previous levels, and it touches on the special personality of Homer Barron. Following her father's death, Miss Emily is a not-so-young virgin, very, very lonely and deeply in need of someone near. But she is unable to find a man from her own town because it would mean breaking the important distance between herself and the society in which she lives. So she turns her attentions to a stranger, a Yankee, a hated Northerner who arrives in town to work on paving the sidewalks in the south of town. But we soon learn that Homer Barron, who resembles her father in his behavior and perhaps also in his personality, has latent homosexual tendencies: "Because Homer himself had remarked—he liked men, and it was known that he drank with the younger men in the Elks' Club—that he was not a marrying man."

Aside from his behavior and appearance, it is Homer's latent homosexuality that makes him unobtainable. A man with homosexual tendencies is harder to conquer and usually slips away from a woman, but it is this characteristic that makes him all the more suitable to Miss Emily, who desires but also fears her dead father, whose portrait hangs over her bed until her dying day.

It is from here, therefore, that another explanation springs for the poisoning of that dubious man and the preservation of his corpse. The townspeople suspect all the time that Miss Emily's marriage to Homer

Barron will never materialize, that at the last moment the man with the homosexual tendencies will slip away from the marital bed of the woman who is going to great lengths to hold onto him. And because she, daughter of the aristocratic South, who considers herself to be above ordinary folks, is actually demeaning herself in her pursuit of a man of no social standing—a hired building foreman and a Yankee to boot—his escape at the last moment from her marriage bed would only increase the humiliation. So she murders him, but preserves him in her bed; thus, he cannot get away and will remain hers forever.

But again, the fourth dimension of the explanation for the murder is the most significant and constitutes the crux of the story, which is told from the point of view of the townspeople. It is here that our moral map is exposed in all its complexity. All three previous dimensions—which were only briefly hinted at in the story—serve merely as background in order to reinforce the motive for the strange murder and all it entailed. Extreme acts stem from a combination of several elements coming together to lend support and authenticity to the extreme itself.

Miss Emily is a very important personality in the township, and the interaction between her and the town's other inhabitants is extremely interesting. The story opens thus:

> When Miss Emily Grierson died, our whole town went to her funeral: the men through a sort of respectful affection for a fallen monument, the women mostly out of curiosity to see the inside of her house. . . .
>
> Alive, Miss Emily had been a tradition, a duty, and a care; a sort of hereditary obligation upon the town, dating from day in 1894 when Colonel Sartoris, the mayor—he who fathered the edict that no Negro woman should appear on the streets without an apron—remitted her taxes, the dispensation dating from the death of her father on into perpetuity.

A crumbling monument. Tradition, concern, and respect. A heredi-
tary obligation. These are strong words, sharp and outspoken. Toward
the end of the story, other expressions spring up—different, strange,
strong also, and very special: "Thus she passed from generation to generation—dear, inescapable, impervious, tranquil, and perverse."

Who, then, was Miss Emily, and what was so special about her to
the town in which she lived that caused its people to see her as a
monument, an obligation, a dear concern, a tradition, and a duty?
When she dies, they all go to her funeral. If we take a close look,
we'll see a lonely, eccentric old lady who has virtually no connection
with the society around her, a proud woman who keeps others at a
distance and treats them with disdain and even scorn. Even though
she is a penniless pauper, unemployed and inactive, she behaves as if
she is the lady of the manor, adamantly refusing to fulfill the basic
duty required of a law-abiding citizen, a duty that is almost sacred in
America—the duty to pay taxes.

In the first scene of the story, the town dignitaries pay a special
visit to Miss Emily's home in order to demand that she pay her municipal taxes after years in which she had returned her tax notices un-
paid. Although their visit is humble and respectful, she does not even
ask them to sit down, but fobs them off with a rebuke, telling them
to go check the records with the long-dead mayor, Colonel Sartoris,
and to ask him about the tax exemption granted to her years ago.
The aldermen, vanquished and humiliated, give in and go away.

This opening scene sharpens the dilemma surrounding the secret
of Miss Emily's tremendous power in the society in which she lives,
especially considering that we are talking about a perverted murderess of the most revolting kind. If we review the most obvious component in her relationship with the townsfolk, we can define it as
mutual distance, she from them and they from her. Miss Emily is
most important to the townsfolk in that she has put herself in a place
where she can be impenetrable and virtually unapproachable. The

Griersons held themselves a little too high for what they really were. From time to time, the society appears to try—but as we shall soon see, only appears—to challenge this artificial distance at which Miss Emily has placed herself. As soon as it looks as if the distance will be reduced or disappear altogether, society rushes in immediately to re-instate it.

A fine game is being played here between the town's society and the lady, and it is impossible to determine who is in the lead, the so-ciety or Miss Emily or both of them. Miss Emily sees herself as some sort of aristocrat with no interest in the local townspeople, whom she considers beneath her dignity. This exaggerated self-image was probably instilled in her by her father, who rejected the approaches of any young men who came courting her, whether out of oedipal jealousy or from a genuine sense of his family's importance. Perhaps because of deteriorated social and financial standing, he tended to "stretch" the awareness of his self-value beyond its realistic propor-tions. In America, there is no such thing as an aristocracy acquired by force of historic memory and the overprivilege of past standing; it must receive its legitimacy not from an external source, but from the strength of the individual's desire, an individual who decrees himself to be a person of position. In the Southern states, where they shunned Northern-style individual liberty, there was special reason to justify racism by stressing a class-based society, similar to Europe of old.

In the great and cruel civil war of the mid–nineteenth century, the North and South fought over the future image of American so-ciety. The Northern side presented a code of human liberty in which man can do as he wishes but is also subject to his destiny, with all the alienation, loneliness, and selfishness that this liberty sows around it in human society. And on the Southern side, there stood a code of racism and stratification as well as a society based on class, which, alongside the cruelty and exploitation that stems from such a society, also promises honor and belonging through devotion to family tradition.

The Southern society described in this story was conquered many years prior to the events of the story, and the codes that now rule it are those of the winners, a strange representative of whom rolls into town one day in the form of a building foreman called Homer Barron. Miss Emily represents the old world, not by what she does, but by what she does not do—in other words, by the frozen state in which she exists. A description of her home bears reliable witness to this point: "It smelled of dust and disuse—a close, dank smell. The Negro led them into the parlor. It was furnished in heavy, leather-covered furniture. When the Negro opened the blinds of one window, they could see that the leather was cracked; and when they sat down, a faint dust rose sluggishly about their thighs, spinning with slow motes in the single sunray."

And it goes on: "She did not ask them to sit. She just stood in the door and listened quietly until the spokesman came to a stumbling halt. Then they could hear the invisible watch ticking at the end of the gold chain."

Miss Emily has her own time, which is not attuned to the general clock of her fellow townspeople. But in order to make time stand still, in order to remain unapproachable to the collective, she must, in an inner sense, become aware of its passing, to feel its intentions, its changes, so as to know how to defend herself against it.

But do the townsfolk really wish to reduce the distance between themselves and Miss Emily, to take her out of her frozen condition and to domesticate her into the town? The answer is that in their own way they are cooperating with Miss Emily's isolation fixation and with her "unapproachability." Perhaps the fact that she is frozen in the old codes of bygone days serves them as a criterion for better understanding themselves, for good or for bad. It is for this reason that they exempt her even from paying her taxes: in her mere existence, she is fulfilling an important public and social function.

The libidinal focus of the relationship between Miss Emily and the society around her relates to Miss Emily's marriage because marriage is not simply a personal act; it is also a social act. Miss Emily's marriage will ensure her integration and domestication into society. Her father's rejection of all potential local bridegrooms was not connected merely to his oedipal hold on his pretty daughter, but also to the fear that her marriage to a local young man would reduce and perhaps even overrule completely the distance (snobbish or genuinely aristocratic) from the surrounding society, a distance that is important to him to maintain in order to preserve his eminence. "So when she got to be thirty and was still single, we were not pleased exactly, but vindicated; even with insanity in the family she wouldn't have turned down all of her chances if they really materialized."

The society's attitude to the possibility of Miss Emily's marrying is ambiguous. At first glance, it would appear that they genuinely wanted her to get married, but at the same time they would have liked for her to remain off in that distant place in which she had set herself: inviolate and full of self-importance, whether real or imagined. "We were not pleased exactly, but vindicated." Here, the first sentence begins to express the society's dangerous ambiguity toward Miss Emily, that same ambiguity that exempts her from paying taxes, but at so heavy a cost.

When the father dies, the townsfolk think at first, gleefully even, that the time has come to break the deep gap between themselves and Miss Emily, who has become human and therefore more approachable. But when they come to bury her father and to express their condolences, and thus to get closer to her, they are immediately shunned by the proud orphan, who denies her father's death and refuses to be comforted.

Again, the collective reaction of the townsfolk is very interesting: "We did not say she was crazy then. We believed she had to do that. We remembered all the young men her father had driven away and we knew that with nothing left, she would have to cling to that which had robbed her, as people will." In other words, notwithstanding their desire to diminish the distance between Miss Emily and themselves, not only do they accept her eccentric behavior and rejection, they even find nice reasons to justify it.

The ambiguous collective will of the townsfolk wants on the one hand to annul the detached, strange, and ridiculous status Miss Emily has taken for herself, but on the other hand to continue upholding it, whether in growing pleasure or fear, with regard to the Homer Barron affair.

There is no doubt that Miss Emily chooses Homer Barron after the death of her father not only because of his resemblance to her father, but because he is a stranger, which releases her from having to join the town's social intimacy. As usual, the townsfolk accept her new choice in their characteristically ambiguous way: "At first we were glad that Miss Emily would have an interest, because the ladies all said, 'Of course a Grierson would not think seriously of a Northerner, a day laborer.' "

It would seem that they are genuinely pleased at the new relationship, which could help Miss Emily out of her poverty-stricken, lonely spinsterhood, but at the same time they do their utmost to hinder the relationship, which is decidedly beneath the dignity of the lady who has placed herself so far above them. Nor is it appropriate for a Southern lady, even after the defeat, to marry a Northerner, the enemy, even if the war ended so long ago. The first thing they think of doing is to force the Baptist minister—"Miss Emily's people were Episcopal"—to call upon her to try to put an end to any thought of marriage. When he fails in his mission, the minister's wife writes to Miss Emily's relations in Alabama to see if maybe they can

do what has to be done to keep Miss Emily in her rightful place, far
away from everyone else.

Thereafter, Miss Emily goes to the druggist and buys—quite
openly—a package of rat poison. This is the first sign of her deep
distress, her soul torn between a will to marry, to have a relationship,
and perhaps to live a normal life and the desire to maintain her distinguished and blue-blooded "standing"—her "honor" and her "aristocracy." The townspeople are quick to notice this purchase and to
understand that the poison is not going to be used on rats: "So the
next day we all said, 'She will kill herself'; and we said it would be the
best thing."

This sentence, which appears to have been said with some insou-
ciance, is actually harsh and cruel. It is a sentence that signals to Miss
Emily the trap into which she has fallen as a result of society's demand that she keep up the required standards of honor and "nobility," standards by which that society itself is unable to live In the
society's eyes, therefore, Miss Emily is a myth that stands beyond
time, and she is thus described sometimes in divine metaphors: "Like
the carven torso of an idol in a niche," or "Her hair was cut short,
making her look like a girl, with a vague resemblance to those angels
in colored church windows—sort of tragic and serene," or "Miss
Emily sat in it, the light behind her, and her upright motionless torso
as that of an idol." And elsewhere, Faulkner describes her thus:

> She carried her head high enough—even when we believed that
> she was fallen. It was as if she demanded more than ever the recogni-
> tion of her dignity as the last Grierson; as if it had wanted that touch
> of earthiness to reaffirm her imperviousness. Like when she bought
> the rat poison, the arsenic. That was a year after they had begun to
> say "Poor Emily," and while the two female cousins were visiting her.
>
> "I want some poison," she said to the druggist. She was over thirty
> then, still a slight woman, though thinner than usual, with cold,

haughty black eyes in a face the flesh of which was strained across the temples and about the eye-sockets as you imagine a lighthouse-keeper's face ought to look.

An idol, the face of an angel, the way a lighthouse keeper's face ought to look. All these fine phrases describe a woman who is no more than a lonely, poverty-stricken spinster, who arrogantly disregards the society in which she lives and preserves anachronistic "values" that the same society has neither the strength nor the patience to uphold. Whether with humor or out of stubbornness, the townsfolk swing back and forth between a desire to leave Miss Emily alone—to let her get married and escape from her loneliness, even if it is to a nameless and low-class Yankee—and the ambition to preserve the myth of her chastity and to pass it on from generation to generation—dear, inescapable, impervious, tranquil, and perverse.

Thus, one might say that Miss Emily—herself torn between the desire to marry the man who so reminds her of her father and the desire to preserve her dignity in the eyes of her fellow townspeople by maintaining the clear distance that has long been determined between herself and them—is left with no choice but to murder her beloved *and* to keep him with her forever.

" 'She will kill herself'; and we said that it would be the best thing." This is what the townspeople think, who are in denial about the murder that takes place in front of their very eyes. Miss Emily buys poison, and they all know that it is not meant for rats but for killing a human being. They see the Negro man admit Homer Barron at the kitchen door at dusk one evening; they (who see and know everything) do *not* see Homer Barron *leave* Miss Emily's house; and they are all aware of the awful stench of a corpse that issues from the house. Yet nobody has the slightest inkling that Miss Emily might have poisoned Homer Barron. This is the exact moment of denial that society goes through in order to confirm and condone the murder Miss Emily commits. (And the reader, who identifies with the feelings of the townspeople, undergoes the self-same process.) It is a clear case of denial that releases society from the need to deal with the recently committed murder. When Miss Emily's neighbors complain about the terrible smell issuing from her house, she is defended by old Judge Stevens, who objects to sending over someone to look into the matter. The way in which the townsfolk try to cope with the smell by secretly sending over four men in the middle of the night to spread lime along the walls of the house just goes to show how determined they are not to delve into what really happened. Out of a fear that they might uncover the terrible truth, which they immediately deny, they conspire with Homer's disappearance because Miss Emily committed murder not merely for her own honor, but for the honor of a society that is so in need of its own myths.

The denial process is so strong and so real that for years the townspeople have no compunctions about sending their tender young daughters to Miss Emily's home in order receive lessons in china painting. They send their daughters to the very same house in which the murder took place, in which the remains of the corpse can almost certainly still be found in that same locked room on the second floor, which, on Miss Emily's death, they will all come to burst open in order to prove their naïveté, their complete and utter *non-knowledge*, to the world and to themselves. Only thus can they continue to keep up the myth of Miss Emily that they are so in need of if they are to equalize their "betrayal" of old values. They send the dearest, most vulnerable, most innocent girls to a monstrous house in order to prove to themselves and to the world that it does not house a monster—and ultimately that their denial is a success.

Still, as I have already pointed out, this is no innocent nonknowledge; it is simple denial. So when Miss Emily dies, they are entitled to release their denial, which they do with the greatest of speed.

Miss Emily has barely been laid to rest in her grave, and they are in her house, knocking down the locked door to the room they had known about all the time but were afraid of entering. So long as the room was under Miss Emily's auspices, it did not bother them, but once—on her death—the room enters the public domain, they feel obliged to force their way into it in order to find what they had known all along: that a murder had been committed here and that the murder had been committed for them.

Yes, on behalf of the townsfolk. For this reason, not only do they not demand that the murderess be brought to trial, they even exempt her from paying municipal taxes. The fine and complex relationship between the individual and society can easily distort moral foundations and completely muddle up people's priorities. People conduct blatantly immoral acts in the name of society and on behalf of its values and assets, but there is no way these acts can be made legitimate except if that same society actively pretends no knowledge of the acts or pushes knowledge (such as the horrific activity of security services in the service of the collective) into the collective subconscious. The more monstrosities a society pushes into its subconscious, the more dangerous and poisonous they are, and it is therefore important from time to time to break into that subconscious and give it a thorough cleaning. This is what happens after Miss Emily's death, when the townsfolk enter the locked room. But while they are busy being shocked/not shocked, surprised/not surprised to discover the remains of the body poisoned to death forty years ago, they are *genuinely* surprised to discover the terrible personal price paid by the proud murderess on their behalf. A long strand of iron gray hair belonging to a lonely old lady shows them that for year after year she used to lie down devotedly next to the corpse of the man she loved, after being forbidden by the values of the society in which she lived to make true the marriage she so longed for.

From a literary-aesthetic point of view, the process of forming a complex relationship with the murderess was achieved through the sophisticated and effective use of two simple literary means: one of them is a point of view that is timeless.

The point of view of the town is that of the townsfolk, but not the townsfolk of any specific period, but the timeless population of the town, as if they had inherited from Miss Emily the ability to freeze time.

We hear the voices of the townsfolk who remember Miss Emily as a young woman and the way in which they had tried to prevent her from marrying Homer Barron. But from the exact same point of view and with the same tone of voice, we also hear them talking about Miss Emily the lonely old spinster. Thus, if we are to try to identify the narrator in this story, we shall discover a collective whose age span is extremely broad. It is as if the spirit of the town in person is speaking over a period of many years.

The second literary means used here with great success is the breaking up of the story's chronology for the good of another order. This order goes from the external to the most internal: from the time the municipal deputation calls on Miss Emily to ask her in vain to pay her taxes, to the story of the smell, the death of her father, the story of Homer Barron, the story of the poison, and finally the discovery of the lone gray hair lying in the dent in the pillow beside the crumbling skeleton.

In this way, the personal and the public come together in a tragic story. This woman preserved and froze the town's mythical time not only by remaining stoically in the house that had once been the elegant heart of town, but also by sticking to the crumbling corpse of the Yankee. Homer Barron was murdered not only on the altar of so-called noble values, which were still dear to the heart of the sinking South, but also as a late revenge for the South's defeat in the Civil War, a defeat to which it had not yet reconciled itself. So this wonderful story moves on from Miss Emily's disturbed soul, via her oedipal-intimate relations with her father and her impossible love for a homosexual man, to the level of social relations and to the broader circle of the American Civil War, in which Americans fought each other over the meaning and direction of their national identity. Miss Emily is not laid to rest merely as a distinguished daughter of her town's population, but as the last soldier of the Civil War: "And now Miss Emily had gone to join the representatives of those august names where they lay in the cedar-bemused cemetery among the ranked and anonymous graves of Union and Confederate soldiers who fell at the battle of Jefferson." The men who attend the funeral—some in their brushed Confederate uniforms—continue to belong to an army that had been dissolved many years before.

This amazing story succeeds in bringing me as a reader (again, toward the moral conclusion of the text, I return to the first-person singular) to such a level of sympathy as to offer a rose, so fine and fragrant a flower, to a cold and proud pathological woman who murdered her lover in her bed and lay beside his crumbling corpse for many years. But on the level of moral debate, I cannot but wonder how great, deep, and terrible the collective's dialogue can be with the individual in a discourse that constantly moves ingeniously between control and noncontrol over denied processes. Anyone who thinks that for the sake of his values he is prepared to permit his daughter to attend china-painting classes for little girls on the first floor, although there is a crumbling, poisoned-to-death human body in a locked room on the second, must also be prepared to admit that the hands that stroke the cheeks of his own daughter have also just stroked the skull of the crumbling corpse.

A Father and a Daughter
in an Unconscious Relationship

IN THE PRIME OF HER LIFE,
BY S. Y. AGNON

Dostoyevsky once said that all of Russian literature emerged from under the cloak of Gogol. With this comparison in mind, it may be said that most of modern Israeli literature was born of S. Y. Agnon's wonderful novella *In the Prime of Her Life.* Indeed, many are the Israeli writers who have pulled threads of gold out of this novella and used them to weave their own varied and various stories. This novella, together with the novel *A Simple Story*—which shares several of the same characters—has been analyzed and commented on often enough and can still be found on the desks of new as well as veteran literary commentators. Thus, my attempt at locating and probing this work's moral map bears no pretence at being general and all-inclusive, but aims only to present another possible angle.[1]

As is our habit, we shall turn again to the story's final pages, where we receive a clear picture of the ultimate objective of the plot. Akavia Mazal and Tirtza are married, and they are starting their mar-

---

1. Among all the writings about Agnon, I have been especially helped by three important works: Gershon Shaked, *The Art of Agnon's Storytelling* (Tel-Aviv: Sifriat Ha-Poalim, 1973); Adi Tsemah, "Double Image," in his book *Naïve Reading* (Jerusalem: Bialik Institute, 1990), 11–24; and "Unhappy Loves," by Nitza Ben-Dov.

ried lives in Akavia's old apartment, to which another room has been added in order to accommodate a married couple. Now, after the initial period of happiness, Tirtza continues with her story: "But not all times are the same. I began to resent cooking. At night I would spread a thin layer of butter on a slice of bread and hand it to my husband. And if the servant did not cook lunch then we did not eat. Even preparing a light meal burdened me. One Sunday the servant did not come and I sat in my husband's room, for that day we had only one stove going. I was motionless as a stone. I knew my husband could not work if I sat with him in the room." And she continues, "My husband's misfortune shocked me and gave me no rest. Was he not born to be a bachelor? Why then have I robbed him of his peace? I longed to die, for I was a snare unto Akavia. Night and day I prayed to God to deliver me an infant girl who would tend to all his needs after my death."

Tirtza has achieved her goal. She has managed to force her will not only on Akavia but on her father and her surroundings as well, and has married her mother's lover. But this marriage, which is supposed to make amends for the mistakes of the previous generation, does not appear to have such a good beginning. Her inner feeling is one of failure. She suspects that Akavia is actually not made for marriage and that she has "robbed" his peace. She feels a sense of alienation toward her husband because she has been unable to separate him from her father, so that it sometimes seems to her that rather than gaining a husband, she has actually obtained another father: "Now I glanced at my father's face and now at my husband's. I beheld the two men and longed to cry, to cry in my mother's bosom. Had my husband's sullenness brought this about, or does a spirit dwell within the woman? My father's and my husband's faces lit up, by the force of their love and compassion each resembled the other."

Although Tirtza is a very young woman indeed (only about seventeen), she is already talking about death and writes a memoir that would suggest her short life is drawing to an end rather than just beginning. If we are to ask ourselves what exactly Tirtza is hoping to gain by writing this memoir, then the natural reply is that she wishes to reach an understanding of all that has happened to her since her mother's death through relating the events in the chronological order in which they occurred. How and why did she go through with a marriage that she herself did not think would bring her joy and happiness? Was the marriage to Akavia essential, the fruit of her autonomous desires, or could it have been avoided? This, in fact, is going to be the way in which we shall examine the events described in this novella. It is hardly a normal occurrence when a son or daughter sets out actively to repair the failed love affairs of their parents and goes so far as to marry an aging lover who did not fulfill his or her original love. Moreover, the deviation involved in the act described in *In the Prime of Her Life* is deepened when placed within the context of the norms accepted in the traditional Jewish society in which the story's heroes live.

Many of the commentators who have dealt with this work are justified in pointing out Tirtza's dynamic intensity against the inertia of the men in her life—Mintz, Mazal, and even Landau. Her name—Tirtza ("she wants")—also indicates her determined nature. Indeed, it would appear that Tirtza initiates her relationship with Akavia and takes advantage of her illness to force both her father, Mintz, and her mother's lover to turn that relationship into a marriage. But from a closer and more cautious look, especially at the first part of the story, it is obvious that right from the beginning, Tirtza's behavior is not at all autonomous. Her behavior is motivated by something extremely powerful: her father's guilty conscience toward her deceased mother's lost love. A powerfully significant moral feeling passes through a subconscious dialogue between father and daughter, and it works so effectively on Tirtza's behavior for the simple reason that it is hidden from view rather than obvious.[2]

This exact region is where we shall try to examine the moral activity in this marvelous novella, the particular way in which Agnon's writings manage to establish the special activity of the moral element (for good or for bad) within his characters' subconscious dialogues.

Our discussion on *In the Prime of Her Life* continues the discussion on Faulkner's "A Rose for Emily" and joins the debate on Dostoyevsky's *The Eternal Husband*, where we saw the destructive power of a particular minor guilt, which overcame all the psychological justifications and rationalizations that accompanied it. But whereas in *The Eternal Husband*, the guilt presented between the two protagonists is obvious and above board both to the characters themselves and to the reader, in Agnon's work we shall look into the powerful effect of moral guilt that floats somewhere in the subconscious parts of the story's main characters.

If I were asked to clarify in a single sentence the literary greatness of S. Y. Agnon, I would say that it lies in his ability to actualize for us the job of his characters' subconscious, which is also the reason why we are constantly drawn not only to reread his works but also to try

2. From now on, I shall make frequent use of the term *subconscious*. I refer to that midregion, that shadowy area between the conscious and the unconscious, an area in which it is still possible to find residues of denial. Unlike the unknown, the subconscious refers to information that is not to be found in a person's awareness, but that does exist in the soul, whereas the unknown exists neither in the awareness nor in the soul. The test of something being either unknown or subconscious lies in its ability to drawn up from the regions of the soul and brought into open awareness—that is, when a person feels that the information was indeed within him, but he really did not know about it. The subconscious, therefore, is the middle ground in which a person still senses how he denied, forgot, or ignored the existence of this or that detail in his awareness for one emotional reason or another.

to decipher them. The characters, their thoughts, and acts are placed before us in such a way as to permit us to feel their additional, unsaid words. The spaces drawn into the text by this artist's hand create within us a state so parallel to the characters' subconscious that our own personal subconscious is filled with the characters' subconscious spiritual material. We cannot quench our thirst as readers in one conclusive reading, but we are tempted to return to the text in order to dig and dive into it again and again as if it were ourselves we were diving into.

Much of the movement of *In the Prime of Her Life* involves this kind of spiritual material because the story is presented to us only from Tirtza's point of view (apart from the chapter that relates the memoir of Akavia Mazal—also written in the first person—which appears as a separate section in the middle of the novella and tells the story of the past: Mazal's arriving in town as a young student and falling in love with Leah, Tirtza's mother). Tirtza's point of view, aside from being limited by the first-person singular, is restricted also in two other ways: (1) the beginning of the story is presented from the point of view of Tirtza as a child, whose knowledge of past details and the history of the relationship between the various characters is extremely limited; and (2) at the stage that things start becoming clear to her, she has to continue to conceal her real intentions from those around her and perhaps from herself, too, so that her unconscious behavior is extremely intense.

I have no intention of describing here the complexity of the novella we are examining, but I would like to point out the strength of the moral element (expressed in the father's feelings of guilt) that transgresses from the father's subconscious to his daughter's subconscious, especially in the first few chapters. Thus, although at first glance we get the impression that Tirtza's vehement efforts to make amends for her mother's injustice toward her lover constitute autonomous behavior, a more cautious read proves that such is not the case. The other characters' responsibility for the young girl's marriage to the aging bachelor does not fall short of her own, although their responsibility is less obvious. Subconscious moral responsibility is problematic in the extreme; it is elusive and defies definition. Altogether, how can we talk about responsibility for something that is unknown? But still, many are the times that we hurl accusations, even legally, against persons who could have known but did not take the trouble to know or did not want to know, and we can even tell such a person why it was so convenient for him to deny all knowledge of that something. It seems to me that Agnon's fine and narrow artistry can draw attention to a new and very enigmatic kind of moral dialogue.

"My mother died in the prime of her life." With these words, Agnon opens the novella. In other words, she left Tirtza when she was in the middle of her life. But the young narrator is also in some kind of "prime of her life" of her own. Leah's death takes place when her daughter, Tirtza, is still too young to have formed any kind of identity or personal worldview and when her dependence on her parents and her home is at its greatest. On the other hand, the girl is old enough to understand—or, more accurately, to sense—what is happening in her home, with its various messages, both hidden and manifest. Indeed, during her mother's last days, in the house that is taken over completely to the needs of the sick woman, Tirtza feels two things: her father's utter submission and addiction to his wife's sickness and the distance that the woman keeps from her husband.

After his wife's death, the husband is so caught up in his grief that from then on, until the end of the novella, it will override everything he does, so much so that his bereavement seems to define his personality. From the very beginning, his extreme mourning is clearly based more on guilt than on a rare and special loss, and it most certainly does not express the eternal loss of a rich and satisfactory love life. Indeed, the guilt pangs Mintz suffers are clear and defined: Leah

and Akavia were already engaged to be married when Mintz met
Leah, but this fact did not prevent him from causing the breakup of
their engagement and marrying Leah himself, thus pleasing her father, who, because of his daughter's heart condition, preferred the
wealthy Mintz to the poor student, Akavia. Not only did Mintz help
in tearing Leah and Akavia apart, but the objective of this injustice—
Leah's health and welfare—never materialized. Mintz's money (his
name means "coin") is unable to help keep Leah alive.

Thus, after his wife's death, Mintz is concerned less with his or-
phaned, motherless daughter than with the guilt that is eating him
up. In order to pacify and appease this guilt, he turns to the rejected
lover, who, ever since the dissolution of his engagement has lived on
the edge of town, as far as possible from the object of his affections,
who married another. Now, though, Mintz makes him a partner in
his mourning, a kind of second husband-widower to Leah. He visits
Akavia to ask him to write the text for Leah's tombstone.

> The days of mourning passed by and the year of mourning was
> close to its end. That entire year a somber unmoving gloom crouched
> over us. My father resumed his work and when he returned from the
> store he silently ate his food. In my grief, I said my father has forgot-
> ten me; he has forgotten my existence.
>
> One day my father stopped saying the Kadish, and he approached
> me and said, "Come, let us go and erect a tombstone for our mother."
> I put on my hat and gloves. "Here I am, Father," I answered. My father
> drew back in surprise, as though only today noticing that I wore
> mourning. And he opened the door and we left.

But what can Mintz's conscious and unconscious intent have been
in taking along his young daughter to so significant a meeting with
his dead wife's lost lover? There is no doubt that there is meaning and
purpose to taking the child, who was virtually forgotten by her father

during the year of mourning. So deep was his grief that he could not even distinguish that his daughter was dressed in mourning.

Here, we are required, as readers, to follow a silent dialogue between the father's subconscious and the young girl's, a dialogue whose moral repercussions will be impossible to ignore with regard to Mintz's role and responsibility in his daughter's unhappy marriage. Why does Mintz take his daughter with him to visit Akavia Mazal? Mintz's thoughts are not revealed in this story, and we are obliged to assume what they are from Tirtza's point of view. Not only does she not know much, but at this stage she is not asking any questions, as if, in her silence, she is prepared to cooperate with what is unsaid by her father (and perhaps unknown, also).

If we try to penetrate Mintz's secret thoughts, we could say that he is taking Tirtza along with him as a buffer in his difficult meeting with Mazal. On the one hand, he seems to be determined to honor Mazal by recognizing him as a partner in mourning, as one who all these years had been an additional, clandestine husband to Leah ("and at times my father would say, 'we the sad widowers.' How strange were his words, as if all the women had died and every man became a widower"). He even goes so far as to let the rejected lover be the one to write a poem for the gravestone. But on the other hand, notwithstanding his guilty conscience and his desire for atonement, Mintz is not willing to face his dead wife's true love without taking along his daughter, Tirtza. It is as if he were saying to Akavia Mazal, "I am well aware that she loved you and not me to the day she died, and maybe that is also the reason that I was unable to keep her alive, but still, Leah and I have something in common that you have no part of—our daughter."

Thus, in order to reinforce himself and his status at this important meeting prompted by guilt, Mintz takes his daughter and uses her, whether knowingly or not, as a personal means of defense. But is this all? Can he also be harboring in the depths of his soul some more extreme intention, not only to strengthen himself in this difficult meeting but perhaps also to "offer" the girl—the living image of her mother, Leah—in some way to the elderly bachelor who lives on the outskirts of town? Is his guilt so powerful that he would be willing to go to such lengths? We can only hypothesize on so wild and extreme a subconscious intention; we cannot be sure. Had Agnon given even a very slightly clearer hint, he might have lost our faith not only in Mintz but also in himself as a storyteller, and the wind of grace and charm that blows over the story from start to finish—in spite of its great sadness—would have been gravely marred. Thus, the textual work here is extremely careful, and the moral censure slips through the folds of the subconscious—the reader's as well as the characters'. It is amazing, after all, that although Mintz is "making use" of his daughter by taking her with him on his visit to Mazal, he is unable and unwilling to reveal to her the identity of this strange man and why he has chosen him, of all their friends and acquaintances, to write the inscription on her mother's gravestone: "Looking at him I was suddenly reminded of my mother, for the gestures of his hands were identical with my mother's. My father stood before the man. So they stood facing each other. 'Who knew then,' my father said, 'that Leah would leave us.' The man's face brightened for a moment as my father's words appeared to encompass him in his grief; little did he realize my father's words were intended for me."

The confusion between knowledge and no knowledge is illustrated nicely in this little chapter. In saying "us," the father does indeed mean himself and Mazal, not himself and Tirtza. But Tirtza, who has no way of knowing the important role her mother played in this man's life, is sure that the "us" includes herself and that the man's happiness at being "encompass[ed] . . . in his grief" is basically mistaken.

But once Tirtza and her father leave Mazal's home, not only does she not draw his attention to Mazal's "mistake," but she does not even ask the simple, most obvious questions: "Who is this unfamiliar man? And what makes him so special as to be asked to write the inscription on my mother's gravestone?" The two fall into a silence, as if they have made a new covenant not to know what they could have known so that such knowledge will not disturb someone else. After the gravestone is raised and Mintz, in a pathetic gesture, places his forehead on the stone and his hand grasps the hand of the strange man who has suddenly become part of the family, the covenant of silence continues to exist between Tirtza and her father. After all, had she known that Akavia Mazal had been her mother's true love, she might have been averse to him, if only for the sake of protecting her miserable father for not having had her mother's love in return. But in his guilt—which, as we shall see, will reach even greater heights— her father still appears afraid of revealing Mazal's true identity to his daughter. Knowingly or not, Tirtza continues to internalize Mazal's significance, so that when she does finally uncover the identity of the significant and definitive love in her mother's life, it will already be too late to remove his presence from her soul.

On another occasion, before they visit Mazal a second time, father and daughter have the following conversation:

"Let us go for a walk," my father said one day during the intermediate days of Passover. I put on my festive dress and approached him. "You have a new dress," he said. "It is my holiday attire," I answered as we departed.

And once on our way, I thought: what have I done, for I have fashioned myself a new dress? Suddenly I felt God stirring my conscience and I stood still. "Why have you stopped?" my father asked. "I couldn't help thinking why have I worn holiday clothing," I replied. "It doesn't matter," he said.

Here again we see a very fine web of a dialogue between the conscious and the subconscious. The simplicity of the text does not tell us whether the father intends from the beginning to go to Mazal's house or makes up his mind in the middle of their walk. It is quite clear to us, however, that he prefers not to tell her of his intention. But why? Tirtza has already visited Mazal's home and has even seen him take his place next to her father at the gravestone-uncovering ceremony. Is the father afraid that this time Tirtza will demand to be told about Mazal's importance in their lives? In any case, notwithstanding the lack of communication and without knowing of his intention (an intention that might not even have completely ripened within him), the girl has put on a new dress for the visit. I stress *without knowing* because during their walk she also finds herself surprised that she has put on a new dress. Is it the sight of the new dress that encourages Mintz to go to Mazal, or was this his intention from the beginning? The answer is something we shall not be able to learn from the text, which is told only from Tirtza's point of view. But one thing we are sure of is that the unconscious covenent between the father and the daughter is becoming steadily stronger. If Mintz's intention is to atone for what he did, he will have to make retribution by presenting—or better still, by sacrificing—his daughter, who so resembles Leah; it would thus be a good idea if she were to wear a new dress, which would give her a better chance of pleasing Mazal.

I feel I may have gone too far, and I should stop here and explain my intention in analyzing the fine and hidden web of unknown material being revealed by the text. The end of the story is known to us, and we are advancing toward it all the time: the marriage of Tirtza and Mazal. I want to examine what brought about this strange and unconventional marriage, which is clouded from the very beginning with unhappiness and joylessness. Which behind-the-scenes partners pushed, knowingly or not, toward this bad marriage, and what was it that made them succeed? At one point, after attaching herself to Mazal immediately after she fell sick, Tirtza asks Kaila, the maid, to take a love letter to him, but Kaila (the only one who has no hid-

den interest in this marriage) is naturally averse to this new relationship developing between the young girl and her mother's rejected
lover: "'Don't foam at the mouth, my bird,' Kaila said. 'The man is
old while you are young and full of life. Why you are just a child, and
barely weaned at that.'"

There is something right in the spontaneous response of the devoted and faithful servant, and indeed all those who have written
commentaries on this novella point out the sense of deprivation in
Tirtza's marriage to Mazal. The question of moral responsibility for
its failure is a very real one. But is the word *moral*, really the right one
to use here? We can talk about responsibility for failure, and we can
discuss responsibility for success, but what has morality got to do
with the free choice of a spouse, whether this choice is a conscious
or an unconscious one?

Am I not placing myself unnecessarily in the middle of a mine-
field?

As readers of Agnon's novella, we find ourselves in a much foggier
region of moral definition. True, there is no doubt that the father appears to be motivated by a good and genuine sense of guilt toward
his dead wife's rejected lover. But does not this motive cloud his
awareness with regard to the fate of his young daughter? After all,
sometimes good intentions and overpowerful moral guilt can lead to
a hazardous path, which is why we are required to do our moral
judging not only in accordance with results and acts, but also in accordance with motives and intentions. In Mintz's noble motives for
reparation and atonement, we can also identify some fantasies or
"uses" that turn out to be dangerous or exaggerated (such as a covert
homosexual desire on the part of the father to get close to his wife's
true love by means of his daughter). Does the reader have the right
to morally judge these fantasies when the text gives the impression
that their owners are not aware of them? Altogether, can there be
any validity to morally judging the subconscious?

I insist on believing that there is significance to expanding on if not moral *judgment*, then at least on the moral *issue* in unconscious intentions, from which so many feelers are sent out toward acts that are good and bad, successful and not. Know yourself, said the Greeks, and I still don't know a sentence that better bears solid witness to a correct way of life. Know yourself and all that is inside you; you are responsible not only for what you know about yourself but also for what you could have known.

Here we can be helped by literature to better navigate our understanding, and literature has its own special way of doing so— through identification. An understanding of the working of the subconscious minds of the characters in *In the Prime of Her Life* can give us profound and penetrating insight into the events in the novella to be better prepared for forthcoming surprises, but also to feel disappointed and angry about what could have been and was not (the Landau affair, for instance). By personally touching the internal subconscious of the characters, we are also able to judge them more correctly or accurately—where they went wrong as well as what and why they did not understand. Indeed, it will be a soft kind of judgment, forgiving in character, tragic in its understanding, but a judgment nonetheless. And here, in our reading, we now arrive at exactly the same point at which the heroine's subconscious joins the subconscious of the reader. We are still with Tirtza and her father on their second visit to Akavia Mazal.

Reaching the town's outskirts my father turned off the road in the direction of Mazal's home. Mazal hurried toward us as we entered. Removing his hat my father said, "I have rummaged through all her belongings." After falling silent for a moment he sighed and conceded, "I have labored in vain, all my searching has come to naught."

My father saw that Mazal did not grasp the meaning of his words. "I thought to publish your poems and I rummaged through all her drawers, but I could not find a thing." Mazal shook, his shoulders shuddered, and he didn't say a word. Shifting from one foot to the other, my father extended his hand and asked, "Do you have a copy?" "There is no copy," Mazal answered. My father drew back, frightened. "I wrote the poems for her, that is why I did not make any copies for myself," Mazal added. My father sighed and ran his palm over his head. Mazal then grasped the corners of the table and said, "She is dead." "Dead," my father answered, and he fell silent. The day waned. The servant entered and lit the lamp. My father bade Mazal good day. And as we left Mazal extinguished the lamp.

The important part of this conversation between Mazal and Mintz is not what is said, but what is unsaid and what is not even conjectured by the passive listener and onlooker, Tirtza. Is she aware or is she unaware of the connection between the poems Mazal wrote to Leah—the ones Mintz was unable to find—and the pages her mother burned before her death? And if she does indeed make the connection between the poems and the burned pages, the smoke of which her mother inhaled before her death, why does she remain silent and not reveal what she knows to the two men, who have lost the chance of advancing their guilt-ridden relationship by publishing together a book of love poems Mazal wrote to Leah? Had our story been told in the third person by an all-knowing narrator, we could have blamed him and his intentions for the ambiguity of Tirtza's silence. But because it is Tirtza who is telling the story, her silence and the silence of her conjecture on this point are very significant. She awakens in us an inner sense of the boundary of her subconscious and her hidden intentions, and prepares us for their going into action. The pain of the two men, who are no longer allowed to mourn for Leah, is expressed in the word *dead*, which they repeat to each other before parting with a feeling of such totality not only because of the woman they shared, but because of the possibility of their future relationship. What does the young girl feel as she watches them, and what are the plans she is weaving in her heart? We don't know, and probably neither does she. She just feels because she is still unaware of who Akavia Mazal is and what he is doing in her and her father's world.

Our subject is complicated. An analysis of the moral element in the characters' subconscious is not an issue in which moral definitions can be easily determined and judged. Nonetheless, it seems to me that the moral element can be a good lead in drawing out the characters' work of denial and the way in which they pass on to us the sweetness of the tragic feeling at the story's end. We already know so far how Tirtza has been primed—whether out of conscious or subconscious intention—to discover the role Mazal played and his significance in her mother's life. We are also aware of the fact that Tirtza actually cooperates by not asking any questions, at a time when questions would be quite in order. We also know that Tirtza is aware of the fact that only through her resemblance to her mother can she expect to attract the attention of her father, so it really is worth her while to be like her mother, not only physically but also in the desires of her soul. "And the doctor smoothed his moustache with two fingers and laughed and said, daughter of courage. And you wanted to be praised. And as he spoke he turned to my father and said, 'Her face is the face of her mother, may she rest in peace.' And my father turned and looked upon me."

Thus, when the time comes for the true and complete revelation of Akavia Mazal's identity, via Mr. Gottlieb's story (with its almost manipulative intention of forming a connection between Tirtza and Mazal, perhaps due to memories of Leah's unrequited love for Mazal and the heavy shadow of her unhappy marriage), the moral considerations and indecision that fill the air with regard to Mintz and Mazal become decisive in Tirtza's reflections: "Night after night I lay on my bed, asking myself: what would not be if my mother had mar-

ried Mazal? And what would have become of me? I knew such spec-
ulations to be fruitless, yet I did not abandon them. When the shud-
ders which accompanied my musings finally ceased, I said: Mazal has
been wronged. He seemed to me to be like a man bereft of his wife,
yet she is not his wife." And she goes on: "How I loathed myself. I
burned with shame and did not know why. Now I pitied my father
and now I secretly grew angry at him. And I turned my wrath upon
Mazal also."

Both Mazal's agreement to relinquish Leah and Mintz's stubborn
insistence on marrying her despite her love for Mazal create in Tirtza
a righteous anger toward the two men. But had she learned of the
Mazal and Leah story from Mintshe Gottlieb or someone else without ever having met Mazal, had this man been no more to her than
some abstract, unreal name, she would most likely have freed herself
of the story with much less pain and much less distress. Her father's
special relationship with Mazal has already determined a place for
him in her heart so that it is impossible for her to simply discard him
out of hand. On the other hand, had she come to know Mazal only
after having first been aware of the Leah and Mazal story, it is quite
likely that the shame and embarrassment would have so alienated
her against him as to have neutralized any possibility of a future relationship with him. Thus, the special way in which the girl becomes
acquainted with and attaches herself to him, via her father's visits and
Mazal's attitude to her (he even strokes her head on that first visit
and says—as adults do to a small child—"you've grown"), without
her knowing his real identity, succeeds in planting her father's guilt
feelings within her, although she does not know the reason for them.
It is these feelings that will activate with such power the passion to
compensate Mazal for his unrequited love, whether or not he really
wants or needs this compensation.

In the meantime, Tirtza is still struggling over the revelations of
her parent's past relationship with Mazal and tries to navigate be-

tween her anger at her father and Mazal and her pity for them both. After she is overcome at the sight of her father asking forgiveness from Akavia Mazal on the Day of Atonement, it seems that her pity is stronger for her unloved father, who insists on declaring his guilt. She tries to alleviate this obsessive guilt by deepening her ties with him, as if saying to him, "If my mother could not love you, I myself shall love you in her place." All the descriptions of the way they sit side by side, she deep in study and he working on his account books, show us that Tirtza is trying to reinstate the relationship between Leah and Mintz, and to make it what it was at the beginning of the story, except that this time with her own love she will compensate her father for the love that her mother denied him.

> At ten o'clock my father would rise, stroke my hair, and say, "And now to sleep, Tirtza." How I loved his use of the conjunction, *and*. I always grew happy in its presence; it was as though all that my father told me was but the continuation of his inmost thoughts; that is, first he spoke to me from within his heart, and then out loud. And so I would say to my father, "If you are not going to lie down then I too will not lie down. I will stay up with you until you lie down."

The repeated use of the word *lie* is most significant because of its erotic connotations. Tirtza is trying to reproduce/repair the scene that took place between her parents before her mother died (" 'If only I could sleep,' my father said, 'I would now do so. But since God has deprived me of sleep, I will sit, if I may, by your side' "). The father's enthusiastic sense of guilt toward Mazal and his unconscious yet endless efforts at retribution, however, do not permit Tirtza to find her identity and her own world outside of past affairs, and he again points Tirtza toward Mazal. The loss of the poems means that there is no longer any reason for further ties with Mazal, and there is no reason for the young girl to visit the elderly bachelor at his home on the edge of town. However, Mintz *decides to send* his daughter to study at the very same college in which Mazal is a teacher, although this decision seems especially strange for a number of reasons: "I had no talent for teaching, but I also showed little enthusiasm for anything else as yet. I believed then that a person's deeds and future were decided by others. And I said, it is good. My relatives and acquaintances were astonished. How in the world will Mintz make a teacher out of his daughter?"

A first reading of the novella gives the impression that it is the young heroine who is in charge of the strange marriage match, her forthright behavior is so much in contrast to the inertia of the older generation, but a closer look reveals that her unconstrained behavior is navigated in accordance with her father's undeclared and subconscious intentions, as well as those of Mintshe Gottlieb and, to a certain extent, those of Mazal, who, although the most passive of the three, still manages to cultivate—albeit unconsciously—Tirtza's enthusiasm toward him by telling her all about his own mother, a strong and independent woman who took her fate in her hands, left her religiously assimilated family, and married a working-class Jew just for the sake of returning to her own origins.

Clearer proof of the fact that Tirtza is activated rather than active can be found in the scene in which she declares her love for Mazal at the bookbinder's shop and what follows this declaration. The declaration is conducted entirely in accordance with symbols belonging to her deceased mother, using the same synthesis and the same code—as if Tirtza has no personality of her own, as if another entity has entered her being. Immediately after the declaration, she falls sick, shocked and agitated by what has happened to her. In a conversation with Mintshe, who has come to visit, she discovers the true nature of her emotional declaration to Mazal. After Mintshe tries in a roundabout way to dissuade her from this match, Tirtza replies with a very strange response.

"Do you not know, Tirtza, that Mazal is very dear to me, but you are a young girl, while he is forty years old. Even though you are young, you can plainly see that a few years hence he will be like a withered tree whereas your youthful charm will grow." I listened and then cried out, "I knew what you would say, but I will do what I must." "What you must?" exclaimed Mrs. Gottlieb in astonishment. "The obligations of a faithful woman who loves her husband," I replied, laying stress on my last words.

What is the point of these *obligations*, that Tirtza stresses so firmly as a basis and as justification for her declaration of love for Mazal? Obligations to whom? To her mother, it would appear, with whom she identifies so strongly, so much so that she now takes on her persona and tries to amend past injustices. But who was it that planted in her this sense of obligation? Undoubtedly, her father and Mintshe and perhaps also Mazal himself, each in his or her own way, plays a role in the dialogue of guilt that fills the air after Leah's death. Now that all the secret partners in the "let's make amends to Mazal" conspiracy are trying, albeit half-heartedly, to articulate their protest at Tirtza's *marriage of obligation* and attempting at the last moment to shake themselves loose of what they had been secretly machinating all the time, now after they have gone this far in fulfilling their desires, the impassioned young girl has to sink deep into a serious malady, to be virtually on the verge of death, in order to truly become her dead mother and to achieve complete approval for carrying out her *obligations*.

Moral responsibility—for good or for bad, for unconscious feelings or intentions—is a matter that is both complex and delicate; it is like trying to fashion a piece of cloth out of a spider's web. What is the fine border beyond which the unconscious wish can be made to stand evaluation and trial? What is the fine boundary between deep psychological need and responsibility for the act that results from it?

The unknown in Agnon's characters is very weighty indeed, and the author's artistry allows us, as if by means of an ultrasound scan, to follow accurately its every move. Thus, the unknown activates not only Tirtza's subconscious in the novella *In the Prime of Her Life*, but also our own subconscious as readers. By the time we reach the allegoric chapter that brings this beautiful work to a close, we feel no anger or hostility, not for Mintshe, not for Mintz, and not for Mazal, who led the young girl to this sad marriage that has no future but only consolation for the past (they married during the week of the Ninth of Ab).

Tirtza's marriage to Mazal is sad and disappointing not only because it is an unsuitable substitute for the proper marriage that Tirtza rightly deserved to Landau, the wealthy young Zionist, the warm-hearted lover with the strong personality, who asked in vain for her hand. The girl's real passion, however, is for her mother, who died when she was a child and because of whom she receives two fathers, with whom the power of the oedipal relationship arouses in her—not by chance—a feeling of death.

I have already mentioned that Tirtza's role in the novel *A Simple Story* is no more than shadowy, but there is one brief chapter in which she appears in the flesh. It is a strange chapter, but one that I believe to be of great significance. Immediately after Bluma takes her things, leaves Herschel's home, and moves into Mazal's home, the text says:

Bluma stood in the home of her new employers and arranged her things and hung her father's picture above her bed. Her father's likeness had faded, his blond beard that circled his face had paled and the ephemeral light of another world floated over it. Since childhood, Bluma had not followed her father. Out of pity for her mother, she would rise up against her father, who sat with his books, reading and sighing. Now that he was dead he was dear to her. Everything that reminded her of her father made her heart stand still. If there was any doubt that she sensed his attributes, now that she no longer had any more of him than his portrait, her heart overflowed.

While she was talking to herself, there was a light knock on the door of her room and Mrs. Tirtza Mazal, the mistress of the house, entered and asked if there was anything she needed. She also looked at the picture and asked, "Is that your father?"

Bluma replied saying, "Yes, it is my father."

Tirtza Mazal looked in wonder and was silent.

Bluma said, "I resemble my mother." And as she spoke, her face reddened as if she were lying.

The two stood in silence facing the picture. The face was soft and sad and bathed in peace. It was a picture of a man whose only complaints were external ones. Bluma dropped her head and Tirtza left silently. From Mrs. Mazal's words, Bluma saw in her father what she had never seen in him all her life.

Indeed, a strange little piece. As a result of her talk with Tirtza, Bluma experiences a profound and new revelation with regard to her father (something she had never seen before in all her life). But what was it that Mrs. Mazal had said to her? Not only does the author not give away anything in Tirtza's name, but it also appears that she does not actually say much. It is as if her mere presence with its ingrained double Oedipus complex reflects messages and suspicions from Bluma's unawareness, allowing her to look at her father through different, more critical eyes. Is this, once again, another example of moral transference from one unconscious to another?

The objective of this discussion was not to add one commentary to the dozens of commentaries that have been written in the past and those that are yet to be written on this wonderful novella, but to try this time to direct the moral beam that we switched on at the beginning of the book at that twilight zone between the conscious and the subconscious, at those fine processes of denial formed by the characters in the novella that pose a riddle to us all. It seems to me that apart from the patient and orderly work conducted on mental care, people have little opportunity to deal with the revelation and understanding of the crossroads in their lives in which denial processes take place, an understanding that will bring them closer not only to their psychological biography but also to their moral one. What good did they do to themselves and to their surroundings, and what bad? If literature offers us so excellent an example of this kind of elucidation, it would be wise not to miss it.

PART FOUR

Moral Development
as Aesthetic Value

High on my list of priorities for determining the aesthetic value of a piece of literature is the integrity of an author in developing and evolving the characters in his story. Alongside psychological complexity, originality of subject matter, language and its adaptation to content, depth of feeling and power of humor, social scope and symbolic level, I attach a clear literary advantage to those literary works that do not stop merely at describing the complexity of human situations, but succeed in importing to the reader a significant development of the personalities involved. A piece of literature that comes to an end with its characters remaining more or less at the same place they started out is not sufficiently significant as far as I am concerned, notwithstanding the beauty and sophistication of the adventures unfolded during the course of the story. Indeed, I believe that the development and intellectual growth of the characters is an objective every self-respecting novelist should strive for. But, as far as I am concerned, a novelist who has succeeded in combining intellectual growth with moral growth has achieved special eminence. The truly great pieces of classical literature have done a brilliant job of actualizing this kind of development. I refer to Pierre Bezuhov in Tolstoy's War and Peace, who enters the story as a decadent and lazy aristocrat, a man who has to be dressed by his valet, yet reaches the end of this amazing odyssey of the war years not only as a man with a strong and observant personality, with a deep sense of awareness of himself as well as of the society in which he lives, but as one who has undergone a positive moral transformation both in his behavior and in his outlook on life.

Could Crime and Punishment have had the same literary value if, after his last talk with Porphyry and the suicide of Svidrigailov, Raskolnikov had run off to America (as he had often thought of doing) instead of going to confess his sins at the police station? Ostensibly, it would have been the same novel, the same psychology, the same characters, the same events. Yet, the moral development that reaches its peak toward the end of the novel, with the self-confession of the murder, is what gives Crime and Punishment its power and its classical stability.

Does the moral development of a literary character always need to be part of a large-scale work of literature? Not necessarily. Witness the short and eminently simple story by Raymond Carver, "Cathedral."

✌ 8 ✌

How to Build a Moral Code
on a Used Shopping Bag

"CATHEDRAL,"
BY RAYMOND CARVER

The story "Cathedral" is told in the first-person singular and, in terms of time, describes an evening spent by Robert, a blind social worker, at the home of the narrator. Robert, recently widowed, is on his way from the West Coast to Connecticut to visit his late wife's relatives. Several years ago, Robert had employed the narrator's wife, who was engaged at the time to be married to an air force officer. She used to read office material to the blind man relating to his job at the County Social Services Department, and they had become friends. After her marriage to her first husband, she had maintained contact with Robert, who was sympathetic to her problems, and they exchanged recorded tapes instead of letters. Her first marriage was not successful, and she tried to commit suicide. Throughout that difficult time in her life, at the end of which she was separated and divorced from her husband and remarried, she kept up her ties with Robert via the recorded tapes they exchanged.

In the meantime, Robert, too, was married to a woman by the name of Beulah, but she developed cancer, became very sick, and died shortly before the main event of the story begins. And now, on his way to visit his late wife's relatives, he is making a one-night stopover at the home of his old friend, the narrator's wife.

In brief, this then is the background of "Cathedral," which describes in the present tense the arrival of Robert at his hosts' home, their dinner, and the way the narrator and Robert (the wife falls asleep) spend the rest of the evening together in front of the TV set, watching a documentary on cathedrals.

From the very first moment that the narrator begins unraveling his story, a deep sense of distaste for the blind man is evident in his words. This mocking distaste is all the more obvious because it is directed more toward the fact of the man being blind than to the man himself, whom the narrator does not know at all: "I wasn't enthusiastic about his visit. He was no one I knew. And his being blind bothered me." And the narrator goes on to say, "A blind man in my house was not something I looked forward to."

He describes sarcastically the moment of the blind man's parting from his (the narrator's) wife when she had finished working for him and was going to join her first husband. The blind man asked to touch her face to get a sense of the woman who had spent several months working for him. He touched her face and her neck as well. The narrator makes a point of characterizing the fact that the blind man touched her neck as deviating from the innocent need to know what this loyal employee, whom he knew only by voice, looked like.

At first, the narrator's distaste for the blind man seems to be based on jealousy of the relationship between the blind man and the narrator's wife (at a time when the narrator had not even met his future wife), although this relationship is described as purely platonic. But this in itself is not reason enough, especially considering that the narrator is completely indifferent to his wife's first husband, who was the cause of no little misery, which drove her to an attempt on her life. In mentioning the first husband, he uses a tone that is perfectly neutral, straightforward, and devoid of any particular loathing. The man had been an air force officer and, as such, had been obliged to move his young wife from base to base, which had only increased her loneliness and sense of alienation. The narrator seems to bear him no grudge, and even after he tells the story of his wife's attempted suicide, he allows himself to sum up the whole matter in one brief sentence: "Her officer—why should he have a name? He was the childhood sweetheart, and what more does he want?"

On the other hand, he heaps more than a fair share of wicked contempt upon the poor blind man and his dead wife, which completely contradicts the possibility that the contempt and hostility has anything to do with jealousy over the exchange of recorded tapes between the blind man and the narrator's wife. After hypothesizing that the name Beulah would suggest that the blind man's late wife was black, the narrator sums up their marriage in a poisonous monologue:

Beulah had gone to work for the blind man the summer after my wife had stopped working for him. Pretty soon Beulah and the blind man had themselves a church wedding. It was a little wedding—who'd want to go to such a wedding in the first place?—just the two of them plus the minister and the minister's wife. But it was a church wedding just the same. It was what Beulah had wanted, he'd said. But even then Beulah must have been carrying the cancer in her glands. After they had been inseparable for eight years—my wife's word, *inseparable*—Beulah's health went into a rapid decline. She died in a Seattle hospital room, the blind man sitting beside the bed and holding on to her hand. They'd married, lived and worked together, slept together—had sex, sure—and then the blind man had to bury her. All this without his having ever seen what the goddamned woman looked like. It was beyond my understanding. Hearing this, I felt sorry for the blind man for a little bit. And then I found myself thinking what a pitiful life this woman must have led. Imagine a woman who could never see herself as she was seen in the eyes of her loved one. A woman who could go on day after day and never receive the smallest compliment from her beloved. A woman whose husband could never read the expression on her face be it misery or something better. Someone who could wear makeup or not—what difference to him? She could, if she wanted, wear green eye shadow around one eye, a straight pin in her nostril, yellow slacks and purple shoes, no matter. And then to slip off into death, the blind man's hand on her hand, his blind eyes streaming tears—I'm imagining now—her last thought maybe this: that he never even knew what she looked like, and she on an express to the grave. Robert was left with a small insurance policy and half of a twenty-peso Mexican coin. The other half of the coin went into the box with her. Pathetic.

How nasty the narrator is toward the blind man, who has not only never met the narrator face to face but never caused him any harm and had clearly come to his wife's aid in her time of need. The narrator never refers to Robert by name, only as "the blind man." He hurls hostility and ridicule on the man's dead wife and refers to her as a "goddamned woman." If it seems for a moment that he has some "pity" for the blind man, he immediately passes on his nasty "pity" to the woman, who had to suffer so much because of her husband's blindness. And after all those crude descriptions of the dying woman, he even goes so far as to introduce the suspicion of an insurance policy she might have left behind, as if the blind man had something to gain from her death.

If we were to ask ourselves what the cause is of the powerful aggression so apparent at the beginning of the story, we would be unable to relate it to the "taped relationship" between the wife and her former employer—a relationship that the narrator knows about and that even has his silent approval. The main cause of all this hatred and anger is Robert's blindness; it is this disability that is the prime object of the narrator's ridicule and distaste.

What, then, is there in blindness or in any other kind of physical impairment (it is clear from the vehemence of the attack that the narrator would have been equally derisive about any other kind of disability) that arouses such anger and suspicion in the narrator? It seems to me that the anger focuses on a moral misunderstanding as to the demands he assumes people with disabilities can make on the healthy. And perhaps the story of the blind man touching the narrator's wife's neck, which bothers him considerably, expresses the kind of mistrust that can give rise to such hostility.

Indeed, there is nothing unnatural or deviant about Robert asking to touch the face of a woman who has worked for him for such a length of time in order to get an idea of what she looks like. The fact that he did it as they were parting shows that his intentions were nothing but honorable. It turns out, though, that the blind man also touched her neck, no doubt to get a better sense of it, too. But here, according to our narrator, the blind man was overstepping the mark. He continues to dwell on this touch, but not because he is jealous of the blind man for touching his wife (he did not even know her at the time). After all, the woman had been previously married to a man who had no doubt "felt her up" a great deal more intimately, and there had probably been others as well. But the narrator suspects the blind man of "taking advantage" of his blindness in order to steal just one more feel, irrelevant to the objective for which he had been granted permission to touch. I believe the narrator is less bothered by the touch itself than by the moral obscurity regarding the blind man's status and outlook (symbolic of the "handicapped" in general) within the system of rights and obligations between people without disabilities. ("A blind man in my house was not something I looked forward to"). This, then, is the issue in "Cathedral," and it is with regard to this issue that the narrator undergoes his moral development, a development that I have chosen to follow as the story unfolds.

Notwithstanding his coarseness and outspoken language, this man—who doesn't "have any friends," as his wife points out to him (and it is easy enough to understand how so straightforward and

sharp a tongue can drive away any potential friends)—does not appear in the story as someone who is unpleasant or wicked. On the
contrary, a certain warmth is directed at him both from his wife and,
surprisingly enough, from the blind man, who refers to him toward
the end of the story with affectionate nicknames such as "bub" and
"my dear." There is in this hero a directness and lack of hypocrisy
that the blind Robert, with his sharpened instincts, soon picks up
and that makes it possible for him, very subtly but thoroughly, stage
by stage, to impart to our hero the "moral" treatment that leads to a
sensitive and significant moment at the end of the story.

In all religions, but especially in the Christian religion, moral
commitment is created in accordance with attitudes to the physically
impaired and other underprivileged members of society. The unique
occurrence of Christ's arrival drew its power and influence from his
compassionate attitude to the fringe elements in society and to society's outcasts, for whose problems the official religion's regular codes
of virtue at the time were not always able to find the correct solu-
tions. Christianity raised to holiness those who were born with
physical or mental disabilities or those who were damaged by nature
(as opposed to those whose afflictions came about as punishment for
their actions) not only to prevent them from suffering society's attacks on them, but also in order to balance out the damage done to
them by God. Thus, it was necessary for their disability to supply
some kind of reason or even message to a healthy society. They
became society's test of morality—as if society's mores could be as-
sessed by its sympathetic and generous attitude toward its less-fortu-
nate members; as if by not rejecting its members with disabilities,
healthy society would achieve the protection of God; and as if repu-
diating those members would anger God. Christian society, including American society, which has a strong religious identity, bases its
natural sense of morality on that same religious Christian sense of
obligation.

Religion is very important in this story, whose title is "Cathedral" and whose narrator clearly identifies himself as a man who is not religious—a nonbeliever. It is no easy matter in American society, where even the dollar note makes mention of God, to admit that one does not believe in God. But with his straightforward candor and unhypocritical sincerity, our narrator makes it very clear that he is an atheist, and in so doing he captures the heart of our blind man, who, having been married in a church (the wedding the narrator ridiculed), is presumably a believer himself.

> "That's all right, bub," the blind man said. "Hey, listen. I hope you don't mind my asking you a simple question, yes or no. I'm just curious and there's no offence. You're my host. But let me ask if you are in any way religious? You don't mind my asking?"
>
> I shook my head. He couldn't see that, though. A wink is the same as a nod to a blind man. "I guess I don't believe in it. In anything. Sometimes it's hard. You know what I'm saying?"

Let's pay special attention to this brief dialogue. First of all, there are all those apologies that accompany the blind man's questions, as if he is trying to penetrate his host's most intimate space. And let's take a close look at the host's reply. At first there's the "I don't believe in *it*." And then, the more direct and truthful *"in anything."* And the truth is, it is *sometimes* hard. There is in nonbelief a certain comfort and superficiality, a noncommittal flexibility, but there is also something cruel about having no faith in *anything*. In times of trouble and personal crisis, people who have absolutely no faith in anything can find themselves left high and dry, facing a black void, with no clear-cut criteria for judging the world. A man who has no faith is obliged to create for himself his own moral code.

And this is the issue in this story. It is a very American issue because the United States, notwithstanding its religious wrappings, is the land of the individual who shook off the history of nations and cultures, and came to a new world in order to realize his liberty. This liberty also means creating and trying out a new set of moral codes. We are presented with this challenge by the bold and crudely spoken hero of Raymond Carver's story. He is not prepared to wrap the blind man, who has come to stay at his home, in a blanket of no-ble Christian charity just because he is blind. And against his wife's gushing bonhomie, he sets about—with his characteristic cynicism and irony—analyzing his blind guest's personality and quality.

Here begins an interesting dialogue between the two. The blind man—who apparently knows quite a lot about his host's personality, perhaps from the wife's recorded tapes—gently and wisely helps the antipathetic host rebuild and improve his rather jumbled moral code, not only with regard to this particular blind man but toward people with disabilities in general. First of all, Robert appears as one for whom blindness is not his main feature, whose disability is only part of his overall being and not necessarily the part that defines his iden-tity. He does not wear dark glasses in order to conceal his blindness, and in his first conversation with his host, he deviates from the stereotypical trends that might identify him first of all as a blind man. He is aided by the provocative behavior of his host, who not only has no intention of taking the man's blindness into considera-tion, but means to challenge it deliberately.

Following the blind man's firm handshake, which rather flounders the host's preconception that his guest must be weak and pathetic, the host begins a cynical and provocative interrogation as to what side of the train the man sat in; if one is to enjoy the landscape on the way to New York, it is always better to take the right side of the train and to sit on the left on the way back. His wife is immediately annoyed by her husband's irrelevant and malicious questioning, but the blind man remains cool and innocently informs the two that he sat on the right side of the train and goes on tell them about his adventures during the train journey, his first in forty years.

The host continues with his small provocations in order to ferret out the blind man's weak points. It appears, however, that he does so not out of sympathy but out of the desire to gain an advantage—as if to say, "If you really are in need of special treatment, then I want to make sure that you are truly disadvantaged." But the blind guest does not cooperate with his suspicious host. Not only does he refrain from behaving in a nonpathetic manner, but he actually bears himself as one who is among equals, and nothing in his behavior suggests that his masculinity is impaired by his disability. He drinks three glasses of undiluted whiskey, smokes nonstop, and then, with great gusto, joins the others in the hearty dinner prepared by his hosts, proving irrefutably that his blindness does not prevent him from showing initiative with regard to gastronomic order and quantity.

But the test does not end here. The host turns on the TV in order to prove that he has no intention of taking into consideration his guest's blindness. Not only does the latter show no signs of unrest, but he hurries to reassure his hosts by informing them that he has two TV sets in his own home—one black and white and one color—and he makes a habit of using the color set.

Here, it would seem, the suspicious host can loosen up with regard to his blind guest, who is asking for no special consideration for his impediment. Indeed, after the rich meal, a sense of tranquility falls over the house as the caustic atmosphere formerly imposed by the host dissolves. By the time his wife goes upstairs to change into her robe, the narrator has adopted such an attitude of friendly camaraderie toward the blind man that he has no qualms about asking him to join him in a toke, perhaps to peel off once and for all that film of righteousness that people with disabilities are supposed—according to his concepts—to wrap themselves up in so they can be worthy of the moral benevolence of the able bodied. The blind guest, who makes such a point of blurring his impediment and challenging his status of "poor blind man," does join his host in rolling joints and smokes with him that "fragrant herb," although he has never done so before in his life.

Because the story is told from the hero's point of view, we have no clear idea of what is going on in the mind of Robert, the blind man, who emerges as a man who is both intelligent and warm-hearted. And because he probably had some preconceived idea of his host, it would appear from the way the story unfolds that his behavior on this particular evening is not completely spontaneous and that he has some kind of "educational" objective for his sharp-tongued host. At the beginning of the evening, he passes on to his hosts a single clear message: "I need no special consideration. I am no different from you. Don't pity me, and don't behave any differently to me than to any other intelligent human being." In the course of the evening, however, he deepens the connection with his host—to whom he has taken an obvious liking, notwithstanding the host's prickly and cynical facade—with the purpose of leading to a more profound and moral understanding of what it means to be blind.

When the wife, exhausted from the visit and the trouble she took to make it a success, falls asleep between the two men on the sofa, the guest, who has gained the confidence of his host and even joined him in smoking pot, makes a point of continuing the relationship with the husband, whose misgiving and animosity toward him have faded by now. He is beginning to like the blind man, not only because he does not demand any kind of preferential treatment or attention, but because—for example—the sleeping wife's thighs are exposed to his unseeing eyes.

This is the moment for the blind man to embark, with great artfulness and tact, on his educational mission. The TV is showing a

British documentary on cathedrals in Europe, and because there is
nothing better to watch, he asks his host to describe to him some of
what is happening on the screen. After all, in spite of the whiskey,
the dope, the fact that the blind man also has a color TV at home,
and the lack of dark sunglasses, the blind man cannot see what he
would have liked to have seen. And he wants to know what those famous cathedrals flashing across the TV screen look like. But the
host, who tries to describe what he sees, finds it more and more difficult to translate the sights into words, and he begins to understand
that there is indeed a huge void between the sighted and the blind.
But the blind man insists, and in face of this natural and naïve thirst
to receive some kind of idea of the pictures on the screen, our hero
senses for the first time the blind man's genuine dependence on him
and his own intrinsic inability to help.

> "You'll have to forgive me," I said. "But I can't tell you what a cathe-
> dral looks like. It just isn't in me to do it. I can't do any more than I've
> done."
> The blind man sat very still, his head down, as he listened to me.
> I said, "The truth is, cathedrals don't mean anything special to me.
> Nothing. Cathedrals. They're something to look at on late-night TV.
> That's all they are."

This is a beautiful and gentle moment, but it is also significant to
the new relationship forming between the blind man and our hero,
who is trying to play down the importance of a cathedral, probably
in order to justify his own incompetence. But the blind man does not
let the sighted man be. The pleasant, rather passive character turns
suddenly active and demanding, and the intractability of his personality, which has already been expressed in his firm handshake at the
beginning of the evening, now undergoes a revival. The blind man
demands of his host that he do something to reduce the huge void

that exists between the blind and the sighted. In fact, he dictates a moral obligation to help someone who is truly needy. In other words, he is saying, "You, my friend, do not believe in anything, are not bound by the strictures of religion; to you, cathedrals mean nothing. But still I am just as entitled as you are to know something about those cathedrals, which mean nothing to you, and you have no right to leave me wanting. You are demanding equality between us, yet you were unwilling to give up your TV just because I am blind. All well and good. Leave the TV on, but I, too, want to know what's being broadcast at this moment."

And then the blind man suggests making a joint effort to overcome his host's verbal helplessness by drawing the cathedral together on a piece of paper. The blind man will lay his hand on his host's hand as it draws, and the movement involved will create the appearance of the object being drawn. Notwithstanding the late hour, he urges the host, gently but firmly, to bring some paper and a pen, and because our hero is clearly not used to using pens and paper, he first has to go to his wife's room, where he finds some ballpoints and then to shake a paper shopping bag empty of some onion skins to use it to draw on.

Here, we reach the climax of this wonderful story, when all the host's moral hostility, cynicism, and suspicion from the beginning of the story change—out of a deep and personal persuasion—into sympathy and aid. Together, they build a moral relationship through their own strange and intimate drawing of a cathedral on a used brown paper shopping bag, just as it had taken their predecessors tens if not hundreds of years to build those cathedrals out of stone and metal. Now our hero is able to understand the black void in which the blind man exists and offers him a helping hand, not out of any external, religious, or social directive, but from a deep personal conviction that the blind man *deserves* to be given a more accurate notion of the world in which he lives. He draws *his* cathedral not ac-

cording to the TV program, which has already ended, but according
to his imagination, because the blind man is now demanding that he
put some people into the picture of the cathedral.

But the blind man, who with wisdom and grace is able to touch
the heart of his former antagonist, makes one more audacious demand. He asks him not only to help him but to identify with him and
to sink into the darkness of blindness as he continues to draw the
cathedral. The hero complies. Indeed, that same person who at the
beginning of the evening declared that "his being blind bothered
me" and "a blind man in my house was not something I looked forward to" ends the evening by being himself a blind man in his own
home.

> "Close your eyes now," the blind man said to me.
> I did it. I closed them just like he said.
> "Are they closed?" he said. "Don't fudge."
> "They're closed," I said.
> "Keep them that way," he said. He said, "Don't stop now. Draw."

Even when the blind man allows the sighted man to open his eyes,
our hero keeps his eyes closed. And this is how the story ends: "My
eyes were still closed. I was in my house. I knew that. But I didn't feel
as if I was inside anything. 'It's really something,' I said."

This ability to realize reliably and convincingly, not emotionally
or romantically, the moral growth of a character by way of real and
meaningful development rather than through a deep crisis or stormy
drama is a fine literary quality. This quality does not require a
lengthy novel in order to be realized. We have just seen how even a
short story can accomplish it, but on the condition that the moral issue is important to the author and that he or she place it at the fore-
front of the story.

Abraham B. Yehoshua is Israel's greatest living novelist. He has long been recognized throughout the world and has been awarded literary prizes both in Israel and in the United States.